MW00979611

HEAD-HUNTING
AND THE
MAGANG CEREMONY IN SABAH

HEAD-HUNTING
AND THE
MAGANG CEREMONY IN SABAH

Peter R. Phelan
with photographs by the author

Natural History Publications (Borneo)
Kota Kinabalu

2001

Published by

Natural History Publications (Borneo) Sdn. Bhd. (216807-X)
A913, 9th Floor, Wisma Merdeka,
P.O. Box 15291,
88863 Kota Kinabalu, Sabah, Malaysia.
Tel: 088-233098 Fax: 088-240768
e-mail: chewlun@tm.net.my

in association with

Department of Sabah Museum
Jalan Muzium,
88300 Kota Kinabalu, Sabah, Malaysia.

First published 1994 as *The Magang Ceremony and Head-Hunting* by Department of Sabah Museum, Kota Kinabalu.
This revised edition published 2001 by Natural History Publications (Borneo) Sdn. Bhd. in association with Department of Sabah Museum, Kota Kinabalu.

Perpustakaan Negara Malaysia Cataloguing-in-Publication Data

Phelan, Peter R.
Head-hunting and the Magang ceremony in Sabah / Peter R. Phelan.
Bibliography: p. 93
Includes index
ISBN 983-812-045-6
1. Kadazan (Bornean people)—Sabah—Social life and customs. 2. Headhunters—Sabah. 3. Ethnology—Sabah.
I. Title.
305.89923059521

Printed in Malaysia.

Contents

FOREWORD

The practice of head-hunting has been recorded in many places and throughout a long period of history. But during the past two centuries or so head-hunting has been associated mainly with the island of Borneo. Often statements and reports about this practice were exaggerated or lacked an adequate understanding of the custom.

In this book the author, Peter R. Phelan, shows that head-hunting was not practiced simply as a form of warfare but that it had a deeply religious significance for the people as they sought to find a meaning to the mystery of life.

The author presents varied comments from numerous writers. The real cultural significance of the head-hunting that was carried out in Sabah (North Borneo) in the past has mainly been lost.

Traditional ceremonies to commemorate the skulls may never again be performed. It is fortunate, therefore, that the author was able to attend several *magang* ceremonies and record so much of the old tradition. Praiseworthy also is his ability to present attractive and colourful pictures of the events and incidents performed during the *magang* ceremonies. For the reader these illustrations bring the ceremonies to life.

This book is a valuable addition to the literature on the cultural heritage of Sabah.

Joseph Guntavid
Director,
The Sabah Museum

INTRODUCTION

In the days of less advanced systems of communication the expression "The Wild Man from Borneo" spread to many parts of the world. People who consider visiting Sabah (North Borneo) for various reasons may still hold in the backs of their minds a vague concept of wild customs and behaviour. But the experience of a visit to Sabah alters that concept to one of "The Mild Man from Borneo".

Sabah is rich in culture. This book, "Head-Hunting and the Magang Ceremony of Sabah" deals comprehensively with one ancient custom from that culture. It draws together detailed and interesting information about rituals that preceded, accompanied and followed the acquisition of a human skull as the repository of a guardian spirit . The respect shown to such skulls demonstrates that the people who observed this custom were motivated by a deep religious spirit.

The recording of the *Magang* ceremony of Sabah by Brother Peter Phelan is timely. It is a reminder to us that every effort should be made to record other customs from the rich cultural heritage of Sabah that may be in danger of being lost to posterity.

Tengku Datuk Dr Zainal Adlin

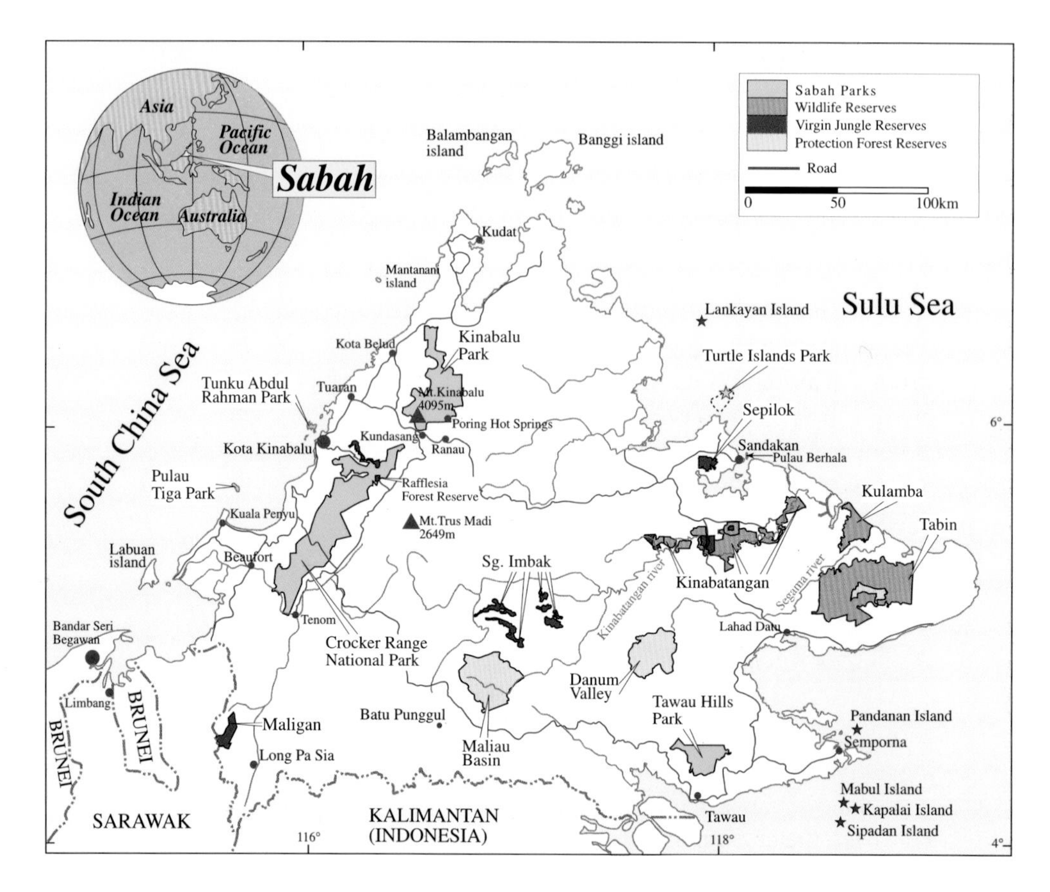

Fig. 1. Map of Sabah.

Chapter 1

HEAD-HUNTING AND THE MAGANG CEREMONY

In 1974 a *Magang* Ceremony was observed in the homes of three different families in the Penampang District of Sabah. Each *Magang* Ceremony lasted seven days. The reasons for these rites were to propitiate or pay respect to the spirits that are believed to reside in the household skulls or to introduce the skulls to a new home or to a new building. The skulls are heirlooms from the days when head-hunting was practiced in this region. Great expense was incurred by each of the three households and that is probably one reason why a *Magang* Ceremony is rarely held—usually at intervals of thirty to forty years—in connection with each set of skulls. In a newspaper account reporting on one of the *Magang* Ceremonies in 1974, it was suggested that there might never be another *Magang* (*Kinabalu Sabah Times*, 1974: 10).

Close to the ceiling in the living-room of a few houses in the Penampang District, some human skulls are still hanging. These have been handed down within the family from generation to generation. However, the custom of keeping and honouring skulls is dying out: in 1976 an elderly man in Kampung Puluduk passed away and his family decided that the fifteen skulls that hung in his home should be buried in a grave adjoining his own, and this was done at his funeral.

Thc Borneo Bulletin of December 29, 1973 reported that a four-day ceremony was held in Kampung Nambayan, Tambunan, to bury all the skulls owned by the households in the kampung. Some extracts from the account will help to show how important the occasion was for the villagers:

'Although the skulls will now be left undisturbed, their erstwhile keepers decided to hold a grand four-day 'removal feast' in the customary manner so as not to offend the spirits.

'The celebrations began with the sorcerer and his *bobohizans* reciting prayers in high-pitched, emotional voices.

'These were followed by non-stop gong-beating, and a buffalo and 50 fowls were slaughtered on the first day.

'Before the skulls were buried, 200 descendants of the Nambayan warriors, old men, women and children, were called upon to pay their last respects.

'Two at a time, the descendants each carried a basket of skulls, performed the *sumazau* (a Kadazan dance), beat the gongs and shouted war cries. For six hours the gong-beating went on till all the skulls were buried.

'There was continuous *tapai* drinking during the four-day feast and a pig was slaughtered on the last day.' (*Borneo Bulletin*, 1973: 10).

One lady in the Putatan area decided to dispose of the skulls she owned by throwing them in the nearby river. The fact that until recently there were no real skulls on display at the Sabah Museum seems to indicate that the people had definite views about either keeping and respecting skulls or of disposing of them completely. By contrast, several human skulls have been on display for a long time at the Sarawak Museum.

Chapter 2

THE ANCIENT CUSTOM OF HEAD-HUNTING

Before looking at the *Magang* Ceremony, it would be appropriate to consider the former custom of collecting and displaying human skulls. It is claimed that head-hunting was a universal practice and was a socially sanctioned activity (Lai Kwok Kin, 1991: 4). "Head-hunting was recorded from as early as 5 B.C. among the Scythians near the Black Sea and as late as 1963 in the northeastern Indian state of Assam" (op. cit.: 4). Some people in Sabah still live in fear of head-hunting; as recently as 2nd February, 1992 a newspaper carried the following report:

> 'Sandakan police today advised members of the public not to listen to rumours that head-hunters are on the prowl. Acting Urban OCPD ASP Sulaiman Junaidi said police will not hesitate to take action against people spreading lies that head-hunters were sighted in Batu Sapi and Lupak-Meluak seeking human heads to be used for the construction of bridges.' (*Daily Express*, 1992: 2).

Many writers and commentators at various times in the past have referred to the practice of head-hunting in South-East Asia but the majority of the references were for the purpose of sensationalism, and frequently little or no attempt was made to see if there was any spiritual significance attached to these skulls.

It is generally accepted that the custom of head-hunting was widespread in South-East Asia and also of great antiquity. Rutter (1929: 181) wrote:

> 'Since the races to which they (the North Borneo Pagans) are allied all practice head-hunting, or did practice it until they came under European influence, it is probable that the Muruts and Dusuns were head-hunters before they reached Borneo.'

A relevant statement by Perry, in relation to the foregoing could set one thinking about the origins of the people of Sabah. He was writing about megalithic culture in Indonesia and in his terminology at the time of writing, Indonesia stood for most of the present-day South-East Asia including all of Borneo. He wrote:

> 'There is good reason to believe that the stone using immigrants are responsible for the introduction of the practice of warfare among the indigenous peoples, who, prior to their arrival, were peaceful. The evidence further suggests that head-hunting, which is the most prevalent form of warlike activity in Indonesia, is a modification of the custom of human sacrifice, which appears to be so intimately associated with the stone using immigrants.' (Perry, 1918: 119).

Writing in 1880 Burbidge (1880: 64) stated:

> 'Even although head-hunting is gradually becoming a thing of the past in Borneo, still so highly are the old skulls valued even by the now peaceable tribes who have not taken a head for years, that they can rarely be induced to part with them, no matter how much they may be offered in exchange.'

Even though it is difficult to be certain about the accuracy of the accounts of the early visitors to North Borneo, the facts put in writing one hundred years ago on this topic are of interest. Whitehead, who explored in North Borneo in 1885 and in a book published in 1893 had this to say:

> 'Head-hunting is one of the most cowardly and barbaric customs, and probably existed at one time in some form or other amongst the greater part of the inhabitants of the world. The North-American Indian kept the scalps of his victims; the South-American preserved the skin and hair in a marvellous

manner, discarding the skulls. Some Bornean tribes preserve the fleshy parts by drying and smoking the head over a fire; the nostrils are prevented from shrinking by small wooden plugs. In the Batavia Museum there are many heads taken from the Sumatran and Borneo head-hunters, which are bedecked with gilt crowns and otherwise fantastically adorned; and so well is the facial expression retained by the means employed in drying, that I have heard that a man could recognize his relation's head years after by the features alone. The antiquity of this custom throughout the Southeastern portions of Asia probably dates from the early stages of man's development, when he first became acquainted with the use of weapons. Borneo has always been noted as the metropolis of this practice; in fact all the pagan population did and at the present moment most of the interior tribes still do indulge in this custom.

'Head-hunting has become, as it were, a pagan religious rite, probably derived originally from a custom of "vendetta". I do not think many tribes in North Borneo embark light-heartedly on such expeditions, as they entail a lengthened absence from village comforts, in exchange for a very trying pilgrimage into the forests, from which the men return often in a very emaciated condition, at times even succumbing to the hardships they have to endure. This custom, as carried on by the Dusuns of North Borneo, does little harm, their victims being but very few; but when entered upon as formerly by the Dayaks and Kayans, and to a less extent by the Muruts, of to-day, it has the effect of almost depopulating the surrounding districts.

'The Muruts go on these expeditions for several reasons, but chiefly to propitiate their "Hantus" or spirits, as well as to gratify their love of bloodshed. Their enemies are the wild tribes inland, whom they speak of as "Orang Tanggal", the Trusan Muruts to the south, and the Bruneis. They cannot however, be on very bad terms with the latter, as I met Brunei traders in their houses. The chief reason for the addition of a head to the ghastly row is the death of a relation, when the departed spirit will not rest until this horrible custom has been complied with. After the harvest is another occasion, this time to ensure a good crop for

> the following season; on the building of a new house, as a petition to the 'hantu' to ward off illness and the attacks of enemies; and in some tribes by a bachelor to win the hand of his future bride. There always seem to be single individuals or parties of two or three on the war- path for reasons of their own; these scoundrels never attack, but hover about the outskirts of a distant village, and if possible cut off a woman or child and bolt with their trophy at once. Some expeditions are carried out, however, on a large scale when the cause is one that concerns the community, such as the rice harvest or an epidemic: then the villages combine forces, and several hundred men go out...' (Whitehead, 1893: 71).

In a kind of summing up towards the end of the book, the author stated:

> 'Head-hunting is carried on in an indifferent sort of way, heads being seldom seen in the houses, and often enough the broken remains of skulls may be found hanging outside the windows in rattan baskets. The vendetta feeling is strong amongst these tribes, and they generally go on the war-path after the rice-harvest, for the purpose of paying off old scores. The villagers of Kiau, Koung, and surrounding districts are, however, decided head-hunters, and, I believe, make annual expeditions. The old head-collecting instinct, however, is still existent, and shows itself in the form of a collection of animals' skulls, including those of monkeys, deers, pigs, rats, etc., which are carefully preserved and hung up in strings, or tied to the attaps in nearly every house.' (op. cit.: 109).

In an appeal in 1884 for financial aid by the Very Rev. Thomas Jackson, Prefect-Apostolic of Labuan and North Borneo it was stated with regard to the local people:

> 'They have a custom of killing people in order to obtain human skulls, which they suspend as trophies from the roofs of their huts. It is from this custom these people have obtained the name of "Head Hunters". But, not withstanding the barbarous customs that exist among them, they have many good qualities.' (Jackson, 1884: 2).

The same Rev. Thomas Jackson, in a letter from North Borneo to London in the early 1880's, described the difficulties experienced by his contemporary missionaries. He wrote:

> 'The missionary living or travelling in the interior of Borneo is necessarily in constant danger of losing his life by head hunters. In some tribes a young man is not allowed to marry unless he can prove his bravery by taking at least one head. A head is required before a person can be buried; others when people are sick; and on many other occasions. These heads must be procured not from the hunter's own tribe but elsewhere; it may be necessary to go a long distance before one can be got; hence the term 'hunting' as applied to this custom. An unarmed missionary would be an easy victim if he should chance to come in the way of a party in search of a cranium.'

The concept of "hunting" derives from the English term "head-hunting". This idea does not find expression in the local languages. A Malay dictionary gives *pengayau* (root: *kayau)* for head-hunter and it is suggested that this word is of Dayak origin. The most widespread local word in Borneo for head-hunter is *pangait,* (root: *kait* which means 'hooking').

In 1927 a book entitled "Kinabalu: The Haunted Mountain of Borneo" and written by Enriquez was published. The author had spent some years in Burma attached to the British Army. We read, 'The head-hunting of Borneo has the same features as that of the Wa in the Shan States, and of the Sangtam Nagas in Assam' (Enriquez, 1927: 124). Later in the same book the author stated:

> 'The head-hunting raids of former days have been entirely stopped, but the instinct to hunt is merely dormant, and frequently breaks out in individual cases. It usually takes the form of a vendetta—that is to say, there is some motive other than that of securing a head; and in this there is at least some mitigation. Three or four of these cases occurred while I was in the country; ... It is not so long ago that a legal minded Dusun came to the Civil Officer for a head-hunting licence!!' (op. cit.: 133).

The individual who was successful in depriving another person of his head was considered to be a hero. Earlier opinion suggested that the hero needed great courage. However, more recent opinion indicates that the taking of heads was sometimes done in a stealthy manner and no evidence of outstanding bravery was displayed.

In "Dusun Stories from Kota Belud", we read:

> 'Kansuring of the village of Rangalan was sacrificing a hen to the rice spirits in her rice field when some men from the village of Sinorob on a head-hunting expedition came upon her. She pleaded with them not to kill her while praying to the rice spirits or they would have very bad luck. They took no notice and her skull was hung up in a house in Sinorob. Later, however, the people of Sinorob considered the head of Kansuring as the cause of several afflictions.' (Holland, 1962: 2).

Another commentator pointed to the lack of bravery involved in the ancient custom of head-hunting. He stated that:

> 'It could scarcely be considered a sporting pursuit, the methods employed in obtaining heads being the very reverse of fair fighting. The usual procedure was for some of the 'braves' to set out from home and proceed to hang around another village with which they were at feud, taking care to hide themselves well in the jungle, preferably near to some of the villagers' padi-fields. When an unarmed straggler or two, very likely women or children, came out to work in the fields, they made a sortie, killed them, cut off their heads and made off as fast as their legs would carry them back to their own village, where they shivered in fright at the thought of a counter-attack. Anyone who had been present at the head-taking, even if he had, as someone once said, 'only danced around and yelled "Hurrah!" 'considered himself entitled to decorate his body with the particular tattoo pattern which denoted a man who had taken a head. The head of a woman or child was considered of just as much worth as that of a full-grown man.' (Evans, 1922: 186).

In dealing with the objectives of head-hunting, Rutter (1929: 182) explained:

> 'The taking of his first head denoted a youth's entry into manhood. It proved him to be a tried warrior and he was then entitled to receive his first tattoo marks. The possession of a head also entitled him to win the favour of the young woman of his fancy and to press a suit which would have been less successful had he been unable to show any such material proof of his prowess. But this was not all. The souls of those whose heads had been taken were believed to follow their victors to the spirit world; and naturally the greater number of heads a man obtained the greater respect was he likely to win from his fellows both in this life and the next. That was undoubtedly the idea which underlay the custom of obtaining the head of an enemy, or of sacrificing a slave, on the death of a chief.
>
> 'In addition to the advantage accruing to the individual from the possession of a head, there were also definite advantages accruing to the community. In times of sickness or famine a head feast was considered necessary to avert the threatening disaster, and the association between head-hunting and a fruitful harvest was close, and probably intimately connected with the primordial ideal of human sacrifice being necessary to placate the spirit of the crops.'

Another author who considered the purpose underlying the custom of head-hunting wrote:

> 'The reasons for head-hunting among Bornean tribes in general seem to have been threefold: firstly, the practice was not without religious significance; secondly, it was considered a sport and the heads regarded as trophies; and thirdly, among some tribes no youth was considered fit to rank as a man until he had obtained a head, the women taunting those who had been unsuccessful as cowards.' (Evans, 1922: 186).

In another part of his work, Evans explained the religious significance of head-hunting:

> 'Apart from the sporting side of the pursuit, where the heads are considered merely as trophies and signs of the prowess of the

> warrior, there is to a certain extent an undercurrent of meaning. According to the old custom of many countries, the killing of a human victim was considered necessary to ensure the success of the crops, and at the erection of a new house a head was buried under the central post in order to pacify the outraged genii of the soil, who had been disturbed by the operations of the house-builders'. (op. cit.: 159).

Yet another explanation was provided by Mr. Anthony Lojuta when he was interviewed by James Sarda (1994: 6). Anthony claimed that while the manhood theory may have been true of the Ibans and Bidayuhs of Sarawak, it was not the case with the Kadazandusuns, at least in Penampang.

> "Our ancestors took heads because they were lazy," he said. "There was no justice in acquiring land those days and many preferred to wait until someone else cleared theirs before also staking a claim. Often this resulted in conflict which had to be resolved through a fight. Those were times when might was right and the 'fair fight' required both claimants to submerge themselves in the Penampang River to see who could outlast the other.
>
> The price of defeat, however, was more than the land and the head of the loser. The victor also enslaved the spirit of the loser into looking after the lands and other possessions. Those who were brave amassed the most land."
>
> Anthony's grandfather related to him many such duels taking place long ago along the banks of the Penampang River where the bridge now stands. The fight would also see *Bohohizans* of both sides praying hard by the riverbanks that their respective contestant would win. "The person who gives up and runs away is declared the loser and will lose his head if he does not make good his escape as the rival gang members will try to catch him."

In reference to two heads that had been taken in Iban territory in Sarawak, Domalain (1973: 174) stated:

> 'According to Iban belief, the village had been deprived of two spiritual forces, and the only way of retrieving them was by capturing two other heads.'

In a comparatively recent study of head-hunting among the Kenyah people, further south in Borneo, the author discounted many of the earlier published reasons given for head-hunting and corroborated the opinion of Elshout who had lived a number of years with the Kenyahs:

> 'Elshout points out correctly the strong connection between the possession of a head and the need for establishing an equilibrium within the life of the individual kampong. According to him there was the need to maintain a certain state of peace with the spirits and this could not be done without the possession of certain objects, e.g., stones, fire, iron and among these the possession of a human head. These objects were supposed to give to the people courage and safety. It is a custom, therefore, according to him, that finds its roots in the religious life of the Kenyahs and especially in their desire for a prosperous existence which is not possible when a man is not in possession of public harmony.' (Galvin, 1974: 17).

Later in the same study we are given an explanation of the religious significance of preserving the heads that had been captured:

> 'No doubt in the old days it was considered an essential part of this appeasement of the gods to offer the head of the enemy. But there is something further than this. The head is held as a sacred object and therefore must be treated in a sacred way even though it is the head of an enemy. The head possesses a spirit which has a cleansing effect on mankind. Therefore it is important for us to remember in connection with head-hunting that uppermost in the mind of the Kenyah is the anxiety to possess a spirit which can only be found in the acquisition of a head.' (op. cit.: 21).

The foregoing account refers to the Kenyah of Sarawak where the practice of head-hunting was a stronger tradition than in Sabah. However, studies of the different customs of the various groups in all of

Borneo indicate a remarkable similarity in beliefs. Where the practice of head-hunting was considered more important it is probable that the beliefs underlying it are more vivid in the minds of the people.

> 'Head-hunting was never so popular among the Dusuns as among the Kenyah Kayans of Sarawak and the Muruts, since they are essentially a peaceable race of cultivators, who have always been the oppressed rather than the oppressors, their wives and children in former days being frequently seized and sold into slavery by bands of raiding Bajaus and Illanuns from the coast.' (Evans, 1922: 160).

Writing in "The Pagans of North Borneo", Rutter quoted from Evans and listed a number of taboos in connection with head-hunting. We read:

'1. When the men are on the war-path the women must not weave cloth or their husbands will be unable to escape from the enemy, because they will become uncertain in which direction to run. In the weaving of cloth the backward and forward movements of the shuttle represent the uncertain movements of a man running first to one side and then to another in order to escape an enemy.

2. The women must not sit sprawling about or with their legs crossed, else their husbands will not have strength for anything.

On the other hand:

3. It is lucky for the women to keep walking about, for then the men will have strength to walk far.

The following were furnished by the Pensiangan Chiefs referred to:

4. The women might not sleep by day, but only at night, otherwise the men would be heavy, would trip, and fail to see obstacles.

5. They might not eat bananas or limes, lest the men's bones became soft and their muscles slack.

6. They might not drink rice-beer (*tapai*) lest the men when running would be in bad condition and froth at the mouth.

7. They might not eat sugar-cane, for the same reason as 6. This taboo also applied to boys on their first raid, but did not apply to men who had been on a raid before.

8. Each woman must light, every night, a piece of resin-gum (damar), and place it on a large stone so that the men might see clearly.

9. Once every night the women had to run, in line, up and down the length of the house and sing:

   Lambai nu sangang, lakau nu mawah, kono intatengah, ke limanan.

Literally translated, this is:

'The flight of the hornbill, the walk of the porcupine, like a straight passage, no sickness.'

'*Tatengah* is the long passage down the centre of a Murut house. *Limanan* means sick, or tired, or wounded. The Hornbill is the bird of war, its flight being typically swift and high above jungle obstacles. The porcupine runs swiftly and can charge straight through grass or bush or thorn without getting scratched and its pursuers cannot follow it. The meaning therefore is: 'May our men be as warlike and swift as the hornbill, as quick and as hard to follow as the porcupine, may their path be as open and clear as the central passage of their own house, and may they meet with no ill fortune on their journey.'

'These taboo had to be strictly observed by the wives of men who were away on the raid, by the mothers of such as were unmarried and by the sisters of raiding bachelors whose mothers were dead. There were no taboo for men who remained in the house.' (Rutter, 1922: 191).

Among the Kenyah of Sarawak, the role of women in preserving the head-hunting *adat* was notable. In corroborating the findings of Elshout, Galvin (1974: 18) stated that:

> '...the women were conscious that it was important for them to see that the spirit of courage was present in the house and therefore, no doubt, the women encouraged the menfolk to become 'ayau' or headhunters simply as a means of finding a strengthening influence in the kampong itself.'

Traditions of Head-Hunting in Tambunan District

In Tambunan District there are at least four structures in which human skulls are still preserved from the days when head-hunting was in vogue. One skull-house is at Kampung Sunsuron, one in Kampung Karanaan, one in Kampung Kituntul and one in Kampung Tibabar. An account of each of these, together with some of the beliefs of the people of this interior district, by throwing a little light on the practice of head-hunting may help to increase our understanding of the significance—particularly the religious significance—of this former custom.

The people here distinguish between various types of head-hunting. They can be listed as:

a) head-collecting as a result of tribal war;
b) head-hunting by a large group: heads thus obtained would be held communally;
c) head-hunting by a small group; skulls obtained in this way would usually be kept by a family;
d) head-hunting by an individual as a proof of bravery: the spirit of the victim was believed to follow the captor to the next world and consequently, he enjoyed greater renown not only in this world but in the next;
e) head-hunting by an individual to win a bride:

> 'Young women not yet married used to sing *"Guntalou ih yanak wagu, amu kosuli bangkai"* meaning "You are a coward—you

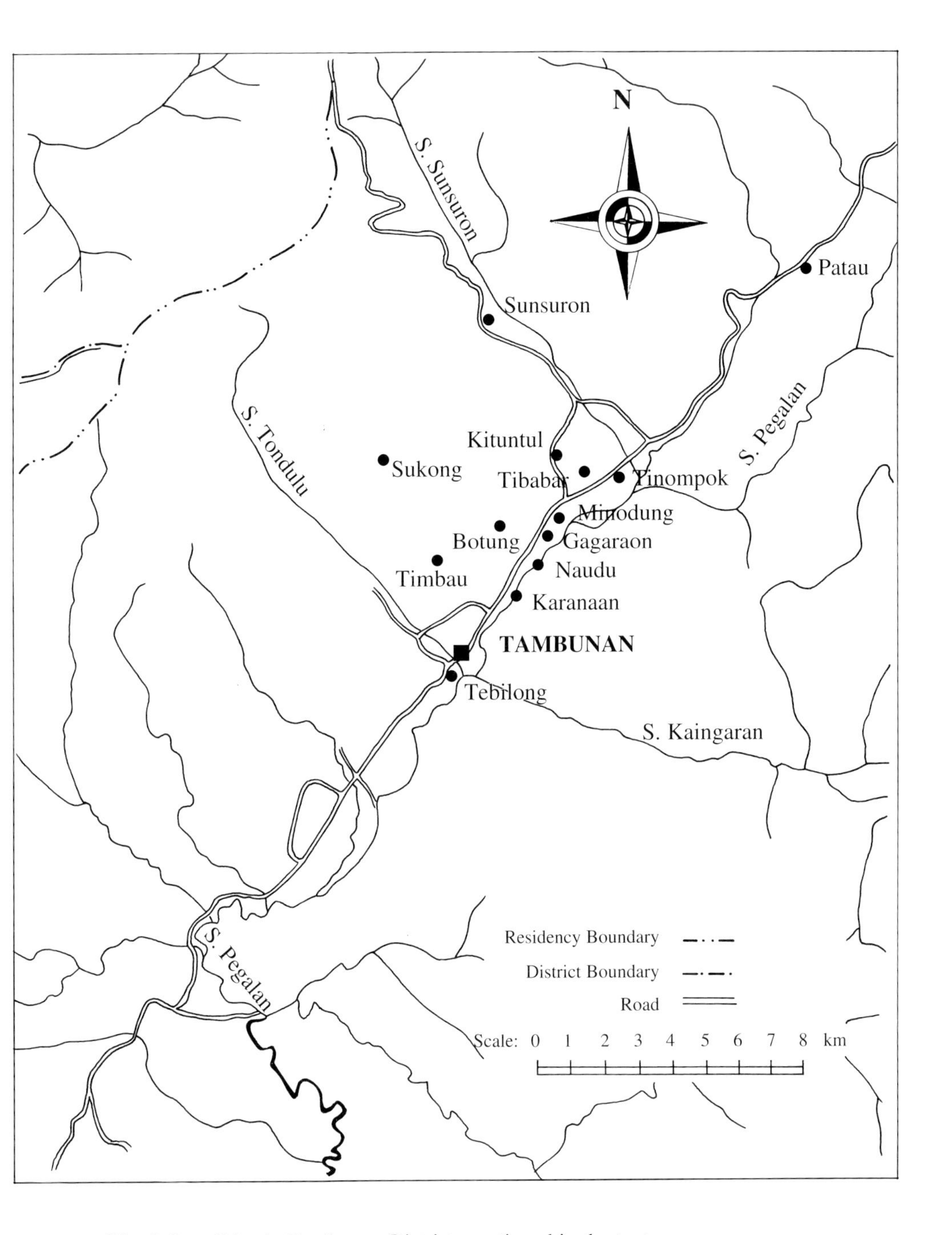

Fig. 2. Localities in Tambunan District mentioned in the text.

cannot get the head of our young men who took away the heads of your young men" '(Joseph Podtung[1]).

f) obtaining skulls for various purposes, for example:
   (i) To put beneath the foundation of a new house in order to ward off sickness and attacks;
   (ii) To put beneath the foundation of a bridge;
   (iii) To ward off an epidemic;
   (iv) To possess protecting and guardian spirits for the village;
   (v) To enable the spirit of a departed relative to rest and not return and disturb them;
   (vi) To acquire the strength of the victim.

Before a head-hunting party went on a raid, usually certain rituals had to be observed. Sometimes the place to be attacked was so far away that the group of warriors would be away from their village for several days. During this time the women-folk had to follow certain taboos so as to ensure the success of the raid and the safe return of their men. However, there were occasions when the men of a village which was being, or about to be, raided made a counter-attack or a sudden retaliatory attack; in such cases there was not time for the normal rituals, but any heads taken received the usual honours.

When the members of the raiding party arrived back in their own village, any heads they had taken were hung on a tree in or close to the village. One tree, preferably a *nunuk* tree, was always used for this purpose and it had the name *Sogindai.* In 1983 there was a large tree at Kampung Pomotodon, close to the main road and less than a mile from the shophouses of Tambunan that was still known as *Sogindai* (Fig. 3). In the west-coast lowlands the word *'sogindai'* is used for a clump of bamboo which is occasionally used as a centre for various prayers and offerings, for example, praying for rain during a dry season.

Reference to *Sogindai* can be found in the proceedings of the Royal Geographical Society, London in 1957. Dr. D. Wood and Mr. Brian Moser were members of the Cambridge North Borneo Expedition, 1956; they read a paper entitled "Village Communities in the Tambunan Area

[1]Joseph Podtung (pers. comm.) was one of the elders in Kampung Gagaraon, Tambunan.

of British North Borneo" to the Royal Geographical Society, London on 13th May, 1957. In dealing with sites and nuclei of villages, there is a reference to a *sogindai* at Kampung Tebilong:

> 'The kampung reserve was once the site of a *sogindai* where newly taken heads were displayed; and the villagers with superstitious dislike of inhabiting a site that was a show place for the trophies of their ancestors, have dispersed to huts on their own parcels of land.' (Wood & Moser, 1957: 58).

While the skulls were hanging on the *sogindai,* people of the village guarded them. No case is remembered where the village that suffered the loss attempted to take back the skulls that had been captured; if and when they did make a counter raid, the purpose was to take heads of the

Fig. 3. The *sogindai at* Kampung Pomotodon.

inhabitants. Several *sogindai* trees still survive; in many villages they have died and decayed but are still remembered. These trees are regarded with a respect based on fear.

After several days or weeks what could be called an installation ceremony was held by the village in which the priestesses played the major role. They formed a circle and danced round the *Sogindai* as they chanted incantations. Later the skull would be installed in the home of the captor or in the village common head-house.

What spirit was in the skull? One informant stated that during the ceremony held around the *sogindai,* the priestesses endowed each skull with a spirit. However, the general opinion is that the spirit in the skull is the spirit of the deceased victim. Skulls have varying degrees of importance and fame and this largely depends on the social status and role of the slain person in his own village. The status of the victim is a measure of the degree of power, courage and fame transferred from one village to the other. Moreover, 'the spirit of the war-skull is not limited to the spirit of the slain person but is part of the totality of spirits of his village and, therefore, an erosion of the power of the village, source of the skull.' (Ebba M. Mujamah[2])

The spirit of the war-skull is alien and is, consequently, a revenging and sensitive one. One might therefore ask, "Why keep it then?" The answer to this question can be seen and understood from among the various intentions that the priestesses have in mind when they perform the traditional rituals upon 'reaping' war-skulls; these purposes are:

a) To overcome the power of the spirit in the skull;
b) To transfer the bravery spirit of the skull to the total common spirit of the living and the dead of the victorious village;
c) To instruct the spirit of the skull not to interfere in any harmful way with the lives of the living;
d) To instruct the spirit of the skull to invite more of his own fellowmen from the same village to be slain, or to support the

[2]Ebba M. Mujamah (pers. comm.) was a student field-worker in Kampung Kepayan Lama, Tambunan.

victorious village to suppress the morale and courage of its opponents;

e) To celebrate and give offerings to their God for their victory in protecting the people from their enemy.

The spirits of skulls taken by means other than by war were as alien and revenging as war-skulls and had to be treated with the same rituals when being received into a village. However, different types of skulls were sometimes preserved in separate locations.

At the present time some people are of the opinion that the power of a spirit in a skull can increase over the years if it is well 'fed' regularly, that is, if offerings are made and ceremonies honouring it are held at proper times over a number of years. When properly respected and attended to, the spirit in a skull is believed to provide several benefits; apart from those mainly communal advantages mentioned earlier, we can note:

a) It could protect from harm the family, home and property of the individual who was responsible for keeping it. Since all illness and damage to property was considered to be the work of evil spirits, the spirit in the skull was a guardian against all such harbingers of suffering.

b) A skull could be used as an antidote against sickness caused by the evil of others. In the past after a person had died, it sometimes happened that a thin, sharp bamboo was driven into the corpse to pierce the heart. The hollow bamboo filled with blood and this was preserved. If a person wished to punish a neighbour, he secretly had a tiny piece of this congealed blood put into the food of his intended victim. The person who ate this would soon begin to suffer from a very distended stomach which would cause death. However, if the family of the sufferer could obtain a small sliver or shaving cut from a skull, put it in a glass of water and give it to the sufferer to drink, the poison would be overcome and he would immediately regain his health.

c) The spirit in the skull could enable the dogs of the village to be successful in hunting. To endow a dog with this power, a man needed a small piece of skull; this was usually acquired in a

> secret and stealthy manner. The possessor of the fragment of skull could use it on his own dogs only. The hunting of wild animals, particularly deer and wild pigs, has from time immemorial been very important as it was one of the main sources for the supply of meat.
>
> The treatment of the dog could take two forms. A tiny shaving from the piece of skull was put into the dog's food; when the dog swallowed it, he was endowed with powers that helped him in his hunting. The second form of treatment was that a tiny piece of skull was burned with some incense in a half-coconut shell and the shell was held underneath the dog. The rising smoke carried special powers to the dog. For a period following the treatment of the dog, the owner had to observe certain taboos.
>
> These special powers gave strength to the dog, particularly to his legs and enabled him to be more successful in his hunting. Also, it endowed his bark with a quality that was able to affect the prey he was pursuing. When chasing an animal his bark would cause the pursued victim to become weaker and, as a result, more easily caught up with. The function of hunting dogs is not so much to kill as to find and corner or hold that prey until the hunter arrives.

It is felt chat the list of beliefs presented above is far from complete. Head warfare lingered longer in this interior region than in many other sections of Sabah; consequently, traditional knowledge of the practice is still comparatively strong. Nevertheless, some statements given by Williams need to be verified. He wrote:

> 'Prior to 1880 the plain area was unoccupied and appears to have served as a boundary zone and cockpit of head warfare for several local groups. After 1885, native police patrols under European officers of the North Borneo Chartered Company established a tenuous form of order sufficient to allow initial settlement on the northern fringe of the plain. settlement of the valley floor along the eastward course of the Sunsuron river

> proceeded rapidly in the years 1900–1925. However, continued fears of head taking slowed settlement of the central and south portions of the Tambunan plain. Those areas, along the southward course of the Pegalan river, were not cleared of primary jungle until the mid 1930s.' (Williams, 1965: 67).

An examination of these statements would probably reveal that Tambunan valley has an older and better developed social history than is suggested by Williams.

A modern-day use for a human skull was recorded recently (Ralon: 2000: 1). In August, 2000 a human skull together with joss sticks and other ritual items were found close to an unoccupied house in the suburbs of Kota Kinabalu. A newspaper report suggested that the skull was being used in a ritual by lottery punters in their attemps to obtain 'lucky numbers' from the dead. It was also suggested that the skull may have been taken from a grave for the ritual. In this case those making use of the skull differed from those of earlier generations in that they did not "hunt" for the head by killing a victim.

Chapter 3

MAGANG CEREMONIES

The details in the following accounts of *magang* ceremonies will indicate that some of the deep religious significance of head-hunting still lingers in Sabah among some of the descendants of those who formerly practised the custom.

A function held at Keningau and called a '*Mensilad* Ceremony' was reported in the British North Borneo Herald of June 16, 1926 and quoted by Rutter. This function was undoubtedly, what is known as a *Magang* in the Penampang district. The report is worth quoting here and runs:

> 'In the days gone by, when warriors hunted heads, newly taken heads were installed in the family at a feast called *mamut.* These revels are no more, but the heads remain and occasionally, when the kampung feels rich enough, a main *mensilad* is celebrated to please the heads and to obviate any mischief that might befall through neglecting them.
>
> 'Large quantities of rice beer are brewed; relations from other kampungs and indeed mere outsiders may join in, if they bring rice-beer with them. Certain guests are invited. The houses are decorated, and in these decorations *silad* grass plays the chief part and from this grass the festival takes its name.
>
> 'The heads are taken down from the rafters and, wreathed in grass, are hung near the rice-beer jars and in the proximity of the gongs, of which there are a great number. Everybody drinks, everybody takes his turn at the gongs, and nearly everybody dances. But it is the women who play the chief part in the

> dancing. They dress themselves up in all the splendour they can lay hands on. Beautiful dresses, decked with beads and shells, which only see the light of day on important occasions, are proudly worn. Feathered head-dresses (*kapiak*) help to add glory. No young woman is allowed to dance holding a head; this is the privilege of the older women and such warriors if any who have killed their man in days now past. So the first two days are spent in the huts drinking and dancing.
>
> 'The third day is the great day. Each family supplies a pole lavishly decked with grass which is carried by a chosen representative who also carries the head. These men are gaily decked with grass worked into hats and jackets and streamers. A procession of the representatives with gongs in front of them dances round the fields while the rest of the people go down to the river. Here the women dance while the men fill hollow bamboos with water. Some of the old women croon songs to themselves. As soon as the procession appears, a wild rush is made, and water from the bamboos is emptied over those who carry the heads and the poles. This leads to some good-tempered horseplay in the river. Soon, however, there is a wild rush by the procession through each house; water throwers follow, but all eventually settle down in the house once again and go drinking until supplies fail.' (Rutter, 1922: 200).

At Bingkor, not far from Keningau, a *Mansilad* ceremony was observed in 1982. This was the first such ceremony since 1952. Two skulls were involved. They were brought from the home of their owner to the community centre in Bingkor. This was a distance of about two miles (3.2 km). The community centre was located at the side of the local playing field.

The skulls were transported on an open lorry which was specially prepared and decorated for the purpose (Fig. 4). A thick bamboo pole was fastened horizontally from the front to the rear of the lorry. It was about 5 feet (1.5 m) above the floor. The two skulls, together with *hisad,* were tied to the central bamboo. Three female *bobolian* (priestesses) stood solemnly beside the skulls during the journey and a team of men beat traditional music on a set of gongs.

Fig. 4. A lorry arriving at Bingkor Padang carrying two skulls. Three *bobolian* accompany and guard the skulls. Gong Players are seated in the lorry as they beat the gongs.

With due solemnity the skulls were carried in procession from the lorry to the community centre (Fig. 5). From the time of their arrival at 10.30 a.m. on 31 July until the afternoon of the following day numerous rites were performed and many incantations were chanted by the three *bobolian* to honour and placate the spirits that were said to be living in the skulls. However, these ceremonies received limited attention in a general atmosphere of vague curiosity. The event was made use of for political speeches promoting traditional culture and racial harmony. Besides many sporting events were organised to coincide with *Hari Mansilad* (Mansilad Day).

A printed programme was produced for the occasion. An interpretation of the design of the front cover was provided on page 8 of the programme, namely:

Fig. 5. Procession bearing the skulls from the lorry to the community centre.

Fig. 6. Cover of the Programme for Hari Mansilad held at Bingkor (1982).

Sabah Flag: The Sabah Flag which forms the background shows that the celebration of *Hari Mansilad* forms a tradition of the state.

Jar/*Tempayan:* The jar/*tempayan* is situated in the centre of the design. This type of jar/*tempayan* which is known *as tiga-tiga,* indicates the great significance of the celebration and in this event the use of the *tiga-tiga* jar is very important.

Rice Mortar: The rice mortar is located below the jar/*tempayan.* It is a traditional facility for the grinding of rice.

Collection of Traditional Items: Traditional items are depicted in the middle of the design. This collection of articles indicates that this celebration is the most important of all native celebrations here and full attention is to be devoted to this honourable tradition.

1. *Tekiding/Bakid:* (Basket fastened to one's back for carrying rice) This item has been used to transport rice from time immemorial.

2. *Sumpitan* (Blowpipe): This instrument is used to kill animals.

3. *Gayang/Parang* (Sword): This instrument is used as a weapon in time of war.

5. Gong: This musical instrument is used by way of beating.

6. *Sompoton* (Bamboo Flute): This musical instrument provides music by way of blowing.

7. *Silad* (palm leaves—*Licuala* spp.): These palm leaves are very important in our religious customs. When this item is used in any of our spiritual ceremonies it is believed to possess many special features according to the beliefs of the Dusun and Murut people.

8. Two ears of fruitful rice: These are placed below the collection of traditional items. Their position, encircling the traditional items, signifies that through this celebration all the endeavours of the people will yield good results and, consequently, all of society will live in peace and harmony.

TAHAP—MAGANG

GUNDOHING DOUSIA MOUJING OM SAVO

Agazo oginavo magahap di ....

do tumindapou kalamazan do **MAGANG** ih kaanjul do
Tadau Koonom/Kotuu ko .... May, 1974
doid hinominon za do Kampung Kandazon, Penampang.
Ahansan do kotindapou kou do ontok tadau diho nokomoi.

Copy of an invitation card requesting a guest's attendance at a *Magang* Ceremony held in May, 1974

(Translation of the above)

INVITATION—*MAGANG*

Mr. & Mrs. Dousia Moujing
cordially invite ....
to attend a *Magang* celebration, which will be held on
Saturday/Sunday .... May, 1974
at their Residence at Kampung Kandazon, Penampang.
Your presence will be very much appreciated.

Fig. 7. The rice store (*husap*) owned by Dousia in Kampung Kandazon.

No government department or public agency was involved in a *Magang* ceremony celebrated at the home of Mr. Dousia Moujing in Kampung Kandazon, Penampang. This was organised by the family members of Dousia, relatives and friends and had the appearance and atmosphere of an authentic cultural and religious event. It took place from Saturday, 4th May to Friday, 10th May, 1974. The purpose of the ceremony was to introduce and install 42 human skulls, owned and inherited by Dousia, into his newly built house.

The new house was constructed on the site of the former home which had been demolished in two stages. Before the demolition was carried out, the skulls were solemnly transferred to their rice store (*husap*) which was situated about fifty feet to the south[3] (Fig. 7). The removal of the skulls from the old house to their temporary home in the *husap* took place in the course of ceremonies that lasted one night. Although the new house was completed in February, 1969, the skulls were not installed there until 1974. The reason for this seeming delay was because of necessary preparation and the financial aspects of the *Magang*.

[3]It has been the custom throughout the rice-growing areas of Sabah for households to build a separate small house in which to store their supply of padi for the year; the reason for this custom, was the danger of fire. If the padi was stored inside the home and a fire occurred, all was lost. Whereas, when the padi was a safe distance from the effects of a fire and the home was burned down then life could continue because a new home of some type could be rapidly built. The supply of padi—the basic and vital necessity—could not be replaced until a new harvest came round.

Fig. 8. The skulls in the *husap* in Kampung Kandazon.

It was at the *Magavau* ceremony held in April, 1973 that a definite decision was made by Dousia as to when the *Magang* would take place. It was necessary to consider the moon, and the time chosen was to be during the moon known in Kadazan as *Tunizan* during 1974.

All of the skulls were attached to a bamboo pole which was about twenty feet long and four inches in diameter; also fastened to the bamboo were old bunches of *hisad* and at each end was a *tobuii* (Fig. 8). A *tobuii* is a kind of flute that is made from bamboo and which produces one note only. It seems that it is made for use only at a *Magang* ceremony. The piece of bamboo is about eighteen inches long and two inches in diameter. One end is closed and one is open. A hole is made in the cylindrical section quite close to the closed end and it is through this hole that the user blows.

In the living-room of the new building a special cavity or alcove was constructed in the ceiling; this is 12 feet long, 1 foot wide and 1.5 feet in depth, and it is in this space that the skulls are now suspended.

On Saturday, 4th May, a buffalo and a pig were slaughtered to provide meat for those who would attend the *Magang*. Six men from the neighbourhood assisted in preparing the meat for cooking. Dousia and his brother, Joinon, from the same Kampung, went to Dimpango in the Sugud area (mile 9, Papar Road) and brought back bundles of *hisad.* They also made four *tobuii.*

Some of the *bobohizan* arrived on the evening of the 3rd; others came on Saturday; by afternoon there were nine present. They were: Bianti and Joimi from Kampung Kandazon; Suimin, Mondu and Onjilin from Kampung Kurai; Bugung from Kampung Mahandoi; Binjulip, Lunsidang and Buagang from Kampung Hungab.

From approximately 6.00 to 7.00 p.m., there was a meal of rice, pork and beef curry for the relatives and close friends who had come. About thirty people were present.

After the meal, the chief *bobohizan,* Bianti, prepared small food offerings in a bamboo container and offered them to the *Miontong*—spirits who are believed by some Kadazans to be the guardian spirits of each home. While the offerings were being made, prayers were chanted by the *bobohizan.* At about 9.00 p.m., two of the *bobohizan* performed a ritual dance called *Miontong's* dance. One of the *bobohizan* was said to have been *Miontong* or rather possessed by *Miontong,* that is, the spirit of the house, for the duration of the dance.

This was followed by general merry-making with the beating of gongs and *sumazau* dancing going on continually until 2.30 a.m.

Sunday was the most important day of the *Magang.* It began with the chanting of prayers by the *bobohizan,* all of whom stayed in the house of Dousia. At about 8.00 a.m., two flags owned by Bianti were attached to bamboo poles and put at the two corners of the house facing the road. They were said to be a sign that a *Magang* was being held. These flags seemed to be ordinary pieces of cloth but they were very special to Bianti: she received them about seventy years previously from her grandmother who had also been a *bobohizan.* These pieces of cloth can be hung up only at a *Magang* Ceremony and it seems Bianti had participated in only four *Magang* ceremonies previous to this.

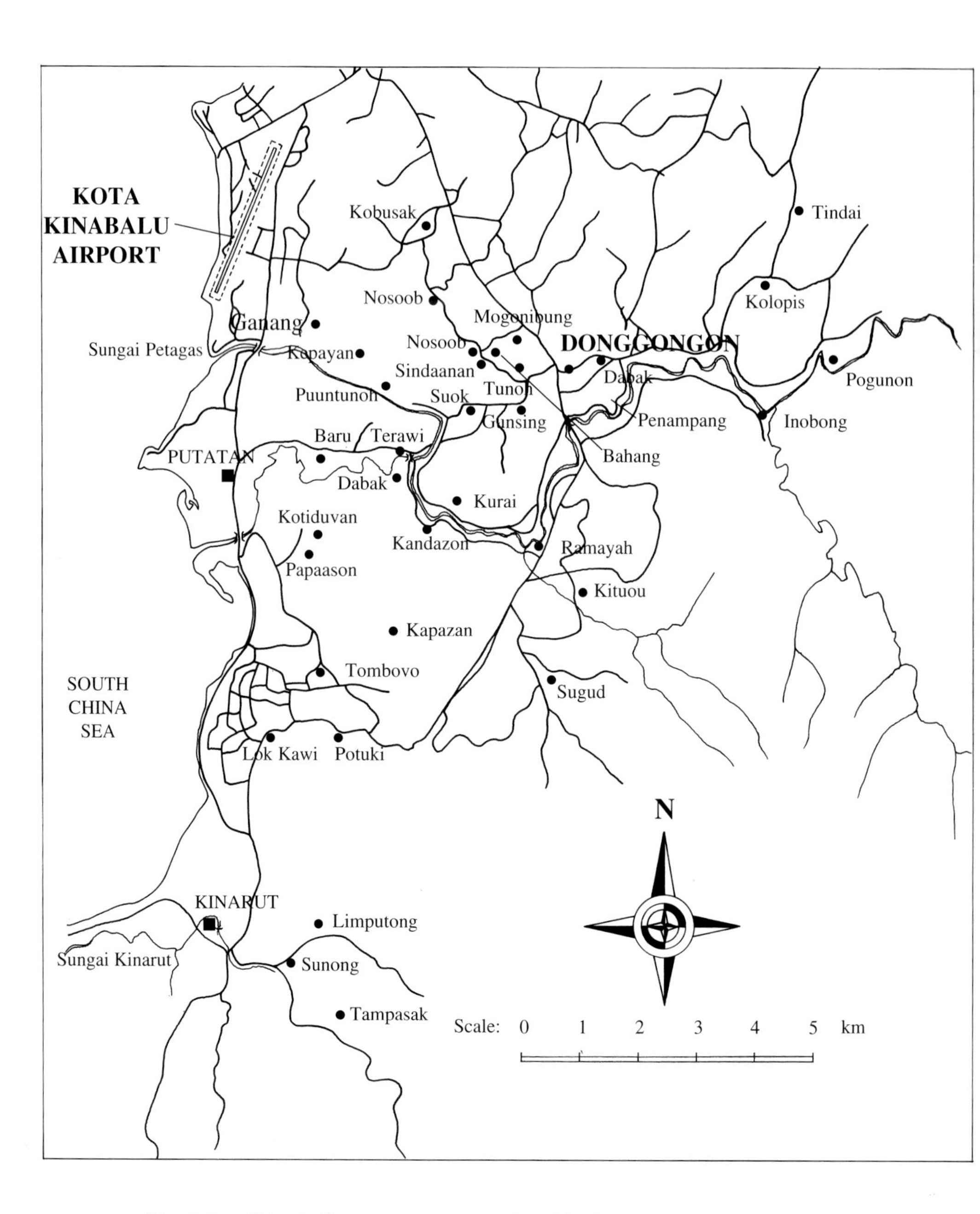

Fig. 9. Localities in Penampang area mentioned in the text.

At about 8.15 a.m., all present joined in a procession from Dousia's house to the garden surrounding the house of his brother, Joinon. This distance was about fifty yards. The *bobohizan* were going there to collect and solemnly carry the bunches of *hisad* that had been obtained the previous day and left in Joinon's garden.

When the procession returned, the *bobohizan* seated themselves inside Dousia's house and began to form the *hisad* into various patterns. The patterns varied according to the purpose for which the *hisad* was needed. Some bunches were required to be attached to the bamboo to which the skulls were fastened, one idea offered at the time, being that the *hisad* served as a kind of pillow. There is no definite number of bunches that should be prepared. Some *hisad* was used to make two sets of *sandangon,* that is, four bunches. The *sandangon* (Fig. 10) is slung on the shoulder

Fig. 10 (above). A man wearing a *sandangong*. **Fig. 11** (below). Young boys and girls also participated in making patterns with the *hisad.*

and allowed to hang down the side during the dancing of some forms of the *sumazau*. More *hisad* would be required to decorate the *vatu* (stone menhirs) at the ceremony known as *Monogindai* which would take place on the third day of the *Magang*. The windows and inside walls of the house were also adorned with *hisad* when the skulls had been installed in their new position.

In some parts of Sabah, the *hisad* is known as *silad*. It is doubtful that a true explanation of the *hisad* in relation to this ceremony will ever be obtained: both Rutter and Woolley tried but were not satisfied with the results. Rutter (1929: 202) wrote:

> 'I have never been able to discover the exact significance of the close connection between the long broad silad grass and the head ritual. Some recent enquiries elicited the following statement from Lance-Corporal Gamotan, a *Pohon Batu Murut* (Pelaun group): It has been handed down to us from our fathers' fathers that proper care must be taken of the heads, or they will bring harm to us. Hence the occasional head-feasts and offerings to them of food and tapai. *Silad* leaf is essential: It is not a mere representation of hair, which could be done equally well by *lalang* grass, coconut of sago leaf; it is rather a sort of medicine (*ubat*): without it, the heads would be angry and bring harm upon us.'

And Wooley (1936: 30) stated:

> 'My Timogun informants could give no reason why *silad* leaves only should be hung up with heads in bunches or plated tassel-like ornaments, and no use should be made of *lalang* grass or coconut or sago leaves. They said that it looked well, had a good colour (light straw colour) and lasted well for several years without getting rotted or breaking up and crumbling away; they noted a resemblance in the name to the word *kilar* or *kilad* (Malay kalah to fail, be vanquished) but I doubt whether one could interpret it as the leaf for the slain. They were sure, however, that if no *daun silad* was hung up with a head the house would be *mali*—liable to misfortune or nemesis, *kenakatu-tula-an*. It was not necessary to replace the leaves on

the heads over 5–6 years old, but whenever the next feast of *mensilad* was held all the house's heads would be taken down and redecorated. The object of the *mensilad* feast was to keep the spirits of the heads in a good temper, so that they would not bring harm on the village; this feast was therefore of great importance and demanded so much preparation and expenditure that it could only be held at long intervals, 5–6 years, and after a good harvest had provided ample material for actual consumption of food and *tapai* for barter for other requirements.'

By mid-morning on Sunday, a large number of people had gathered to witness the highlights of the ceremony. Five hundred invitation cards had been printed in Kadazan. Of these 450 had been distributed. Later it was estimated that 500 people attended the *Magang*; about 250 of these would be considered as relatives.

At 11.15 a.m., the ceremony of transferring the skulls from their temporary resting place in the *husap* to their permanent place in Dousia's house commenced. The *bobohizan* led the way to the skulls chanting prayers as they went. They were dressed in their finest ceremonial regalia—long black dress with tiny bells attached to them; two rows of brass rings (*tangkong*) around the waist; two sashes (*husob*), one on each shoulder and crossing to the other side of the body. Bianti wore a girdle of silver coins (*himpogot*). One of the *bobohizan* sprinkled white rice as the procession proceeded to the *husap;* this was intended as a gift for good spirits. A man carried two pieces of burning dried sago palm frond (*kumba*) which were needed in order to prevent evil spirits from mixing with the good spirits and possibly causing disturbance during the *Magang*. One young man carried a kettle of water and a curious observer might wonder what the significance of this might be. It had nothing to do with the ceremony. The water was used to extinguish the fallen embers from the burning *sago* palm frond—a reminder of how careful these people must be about fire.

The *bobohizan* and a small number of men wearing Kadazan costume climbed into the *husap* and after some chanting of prayers, the bamboo to which the skulls were tied was unfastened and carried out. The bamboo, which was old, was in danger of cracking about one-quarter of

Fig. 12 (above). Carrying the skulls from the *husap* to the new house. **Fig. 13** (below). Allowing the skulls to dance on arrival inside the new house.

its length from one end; a bystander supported it where the bend showed, and the procession with the skulls proceeded (Fig. 12).

The two men assigned to carry the skulls were Dousia and a relative from Kampung Hubah named Disimond. Both wore Kadazan costume and Dousia carried a ceremonial sword in a scabbard. Disimond supported the front section of the bamboo and Dousia the rear. The *bobohizan* followed behind and five of them were fanning with winnows in order to keep away any evil spirits.

With great rejoicing the skulls were carried up the stairs to their new home. Those carrying them performed a dance in step with the beating of the gongs while the bamboo was still on their shoulders (Fig. 13). Then each end of the bamboo to which the skulls were attached was placed on an upturned *tadang* (long basket carried on the back) so that the skulls were two to three feet above floor-level. Many of those present danced the *sumazau,* but the room was too crowded for much freedom of movement. The *bobohizan* seemed to be unperturbed by all the excitement and proceeded continuously with their chanting of prayers.

An excellent meal was next served in the open space beneath the house. While waiting, there was a large variety of drinks handed round: soft drinks, soft drink with a little *hiing* added, beer, stout, *hiing, tapai,* and *arak* (rice wine). Before the food was put on the table Suimin, a daughter of Bianti and a *bobohizan,* sprinkled all present with *bokis*—lustral water.

After the meal, the *bobohizan* walked back and forth within the room chanting prayers and one of them continuously rang the small cymbals called *sindavang.* This part of the paraphernalia of the *bobohizan* is used in order to attract the attention of the spirits and to help the *bobohizan* to concentrate on the prayers they are saying. Some believed that a spirit named *Divato* lives inside the *sindavang* (Fig. 14)

At about 2.15 p.m., many people again crowded upstairs to observe a dance called *Mingku'ung*. This was performed entirely by men. For this dance, about eight persons form a circle and each one rests his arms on the shoulders of those on either side of him. They danced to the beat of

Fig. 14 (above). Priestess using the *sindavang* while chanting. **Fig. 15** (below). The *mingku'ung* dance in progress.

the gongs and as they danced one or more others, while placing their hands on the shoulders of two men, try to jump over the arms of the dancing men into the centre of the circle (Fig. 15). No one succeeded but this created a great deal of fun and excitement. It seems that the *mingku'ung* is performed during a *Magang* ceremony only. Guests danced the *sumazau* throughout the evening. The *mingku'ung* was again danced at 8.30 p.m. by both a group of men and by a group of women. At least one lady succeeded in jumping into the centre of the circle during their performance. The general celebration went on until 2.00 a.m. During the afternoon as an aside, there was some card-playing for money among some of the guests; this is now fairly common practice at such gatherings as weddings and funerals.

Monday, 6th May began with the sacrificial killing of a pig. The blood was kept and later put into two bamboo containers (*hangod*). This blood would be poured on two stone menhirs in the afternoon. The flesh of the slaughtered pig was prepared for cooking. Further chanting of prayers by the *bobohizan* was done periodically during the afternoon and they continued to prepare the *hisad* for its various uses. After lunch, there was some *sumazau* while some men fired the two cannons that were beneath the house; they used carbide (Fig. 17).

Fig. 16 (Left). Making decorations from the *hisad*. **Fig. 17** (right). Firing a cannon.

At 2.30 p.m., there was a *monogindai:* two menhirs were visited, prayers were chanted and sacrifices were offered. The procession from the house of Dousia was led by a person carrying one of the flags used during the *Magang;* then followed by seven *bobohizan* chanting prayers; Bianti, the chief *bobohizan,* sprinkled a few handfuls of white rice along the way (Fig. 18). Two men blew on the *tobuii* (whistles or flutes made of bamboo). Two gongs and a drum were carried along and beaten as the group proceeded. Some carried bunches of *hisad* and others carried four pieces of white cloth.

One woman carried two bamboo stems which held the blood of the pig that had been killed that morning (Fig. 19). A jar of *tapai* (with a capacity of about three gallons) was also brought along. There was cooked rice and cooked pork of the sacrificed pig. Dousia wore Kadazan ceremonial dress and from his left shoulder hung a sword in a scabbard. The other members of the family, relatives and friends joined in and made the procession look impressive.

Fig. 18. White rice was sprinkled to the spirits.

Fig. 19. Sacrificial blood was carried in a bamboo container.

The first menhir visited was *Gintutun Do Mohoing* which means 'the contemplation of people who die without children.' It is about fifty yards across the road from Dousia's house and is situated on a small hillock above the river. The menhir is standing upright and its flat top is 5 feet 8 inches (1.73 m) above the ground. A piece of the stone measuring 24 inches (60 cm) in height was broken off and is now lying beside it; this occurred when a large tree fell across the menhir.

Prayers, known as *momihin,* were chanted to the spirit which was believed to reside in the stone: these prayers were to request the spirit not to cause any harm to the people present. Meanwhile, two men performed the Kadazan form of martial art known as the *batambul.* As the *bobohizan* chanted the prayers one of their senior members, Binjulip, approached the menhir and stuck a *parang* in the earth a few inches away from the stone. She did this in two places on either side of the stone; these were the places where the upright pieces of bamboo carrying the *hisad* and white cloth were to be put. She also placed a bunch of *hisad* at the menhir, this was repeated three times round the monument.

Two pieces of branched, dry bamboo slightly taller than the menhir had a bunch of *hisad* and a piece of white cloth appoximately 18 inches by 6 inches (46 cm by 15 cm) attached to each. The two pieces of bamboo were placed beside the menhir and held there for some time so that the *hisad* and white cloth were a couple of feet above the top of the menhir. Then Dousia's brother, Joinon, climbed on top of the monument and ceremoniously poured one bamboo container of blood on the stone. As is required, he then jumped down. Apart from the sacrificial significance of the blood, this ceremony seems to be associated with the early custom of hanging new heads on these stones after a successful head-hunting expedition. The person cannot climb down but must jump off so as to avoid the possibility of being harmed by the spirit of the stone as he descends.

Dousia and his step-brother individually climbed the menhir and jumped off in similar fashion (Fig. 20). Then the two bamboos to which the *hisad* and white cloth were attached were fastened with thin wire to the menhir (Fig. 21). The *bobohizan* scattered some rice around the monument and also poured a little *tapai* on the side of it. Some of the cooked pork of the sacrificed pig was eaten by the *bobohizan,* but this was done in turns or relays as there was non-stop chanting of prayers. The two pieces of white cloth are known as *tunggu*; the cloth must be white and its purpose is to indicate that the monument has been visited during a *Magang*.

Towards the end of the ceremony, Bianti stood successively on four sides of the menhir and with her back to it, chanted some prayers away from it. As she did so, she sprinkled a few handfuls of dry, uncooked, white rice on the ground in front of her.

Then the group formed into a procession again and moved back past the house to another menhir. This monument is situated about one hundred yards from Dousia's house and is at the meeting place of three padi-fields and an enclosed pasture field for buffaloes. The top of the

Fig. 20 (left). A leap from the top of a menhir. **Fig. 21** (right). Two pieces of white cloth (*tunggu*) were hung on two bamboo poles which were fastened to the menhir.

Fig. 22 (above). Visiting the menhir named *Sinogindai.* **Fig. 23** (below). Relaxation at the end of the ceremony.

Fig. 24. Pouring blood on a menhir.

menhir is 9 feet 6 inches (2.9 m) above the level of the padi-field; it is one of the tallest known and its name is *Sinogindai* (Fig. 22). The rituals performed here were identical with those carried out at the first menhir except that in this case only one man climbed the stone and poured the blood of the sacrificed pig on it (Fig. 24). He was a young and energetic man named Willie Dohuyu, a son-in-law of Bianti. It is not everyone who could stand on the sloping narrow top of such a high stone and then jump onto ground that was dry, hard and uneven.

All the pork and rice taken to the menhir must be consumed by the *bobohizan*—none of it can be taken back to the house; even if it rains the *bobohizan* must remain there till they have consumed the food. This was duly done and the group, after some delay for photography, returned to the house at about 5.30 p.m. (Fig. 23). Later there was *sumazau,* and chanting by the *bobohizan* continued through most of the night. The practice of pouring or sprinkling the blood of an animal that has been sacrificed can be found in many instances throughout history. In a directive to the people of Israel it was stipulated:

> 'You are to bring the bull in front of the Tent of Meeting. Aaron and his sons are to lay their hands on its head. Kill the bull there before Yahweh at the entrance to the Tent of Meeting. Then take some of its blood and with your finger put it on the horns of the altar. Next, pour out the rest of the blood at the foot of the altar.' (Exodus, 29: 10–12.)

In another place in the Bible we read:

> 'Say to the people of Israel that they are to bring you a red cow which has never been made to work. You will give it to Eleazar the priest so that it may be taken outside the camp and slaughtered in his presence. Then Eleazar the priest is to take some of the cow's blood on his finger, and sprinkle this blood

> seven times towards the entrance to the Tent of Meeting.' (Numbers, 19: 2b-4.)'

Frequently the pouring or sprinkling of blood as recorded in the Bible was associated with the making of an agreement but St. Paul, the apostle, points to the use of blood also as a prerequisite for forgiveness. He wrote:

> 'Moses proclaimed to the assembled people all the commandments of the Law; then he took the blood of bulls and goats and mixed it with water, hyssop and red wool, and sprinkled the book of the covenant and the people sayings: 'This is the blood of the covenant that God commanded you.' In the same way he sprinkled with blood the sanctuary and all the objects of the ritual. According to the Law, almost all cleansings have to be performed with blood; there is no forgiveness without the shedding of blood.' (Hebrews, 9: 19–22).

The morning of Tuesday, 7th May was spent in tying the *hisad* on the new bamboo pole to which the skulls would be attached. By about 3.30 p.m. all was ready for the ceremony of placing the skulls in the special compartment in the ceiling of the new house. Dousia, in Kadazan costume and wearing a ceremonial sword and another man placed each

Fig. 25. Placing the skulls in their new location.

end of the bamboo bearing the skulls on their shoulders and performed a dance (Fig. 26). When this was over, a step-ladder was made use of to insert the new bamboo in the metal holders attached to the ceiling so that the skulls fitted neatly into the recess made for them (Fig. 25). Meanwhile four of the *bobohizan* vigorously waved winnows, seemingly to contain the spirits in the skulls in case they might leave them and cause harm to any of the bystanders.

Four men and four women then danced the *sumazau* (Fig. 27). Next Bianti unsheathed a ceremonial sword

Fig. 26 (above). A winnow was waved to ensure that spirits did not leave the skulls. **Fig. 27** (below). A dance that followed the installing of the skulls. **Fig. 28** (right). The skulls in their new resting place.

and performed a dance. As she danced she moved the sword in imitation of the style of the head-hunting warriors of old. During this performance the spirits of the skulls are believed to possess her. She trembled and shook and this was an indication to the onlookers that she was actually possessed. At the end of the vigorous dance Bianti sat down exhausted. Then followed a general rest for all that lasted nearly two hours.

At one end of the cavity where the skulls were put, there was hanging a bunch of the tops of the *nibong* palm. This particular *nibong* palm had branched and this is regarded as being very lucky. It had been kept by the family for many years probably about fifty. The lower part of the *nibong* was wrapped round with coloured oil-cloth, such as is sometimes used to cover tables. It is simply hung in the house and no ceremonies are held in respect to it. The spirit *Tompuvan,* the king of all spirits who is said to inhabit the bayan tree (*nunuk*), is believed to reside in this *nibong* palm also.

Another point of interest was that there was a bone, probably the bone of an arm, which was kept with the skulls and seemingly accorded the same respect. The story of this bone is worth recording. Long ago there was a hero named Gantang who lived in Minintod near Inanam. He heard that there was another hero, Monsopiad by name, who resided at Kampung Kurai.

Gantang wanted to eliminate this man, Monsopiad, who had a high reputation for strength and courage. He felt that the best course of action to take would be to organize a celebration and to invite Monsopiad to it; then he would devise means to show that he was greater. The celebration was duly organized and a messenger was sent to invite Monsopiad to the festivities.

Monsopiad accepted the invitation in all trust. When he set out for the home of Gantang he took with him seven small boys, but before he reached his final destination he asked the seven boys to stay behind a small hill near the home of Gantang and he went on alone. When he arrived he was warmly welcomed by Gantang and invited to sit down. Then Gantang asked one of his followers to provide each of them with a jar of *tapai* to drink.

After they had drunk the two jars of *tapai,* Gantang asked Monsopiad to break a *nibong* with his bare hand. Monsopiad suggested that Gantang should have a try first. So Gantang struck it with his fist but only a slight crack appeared in the *nibong* palm. Now Monsopiad took a turn; he struck a fresh piece of *nibong* palm and it was broken in pieces. Gantang felt that this was a defeat for him but he still had hopes of proving himself greater than Monsopiad.

Gantang invited Monsopiad to dance the *sumazau* but Monsopiad again declined and asked his host to dance first. Then Gantang chose seven girls to do the *sumazau* with him. He shouted the *pangkis* and sprang upwards during the dance with such enthusiasm that his head touched the roof of the house. He caused five of the girls to faint. Next it was Monsopiad's turn to do the *sumazau* dance and he was also partnered by seven young girls. He shouted the *pangkis* and danced with such vigour that his head not only touched the roof but went through it; and six of the girls fainted.

Although Gantang felt very disappointed, he did not pretend to be upset in any way. He invited Monsopiad to have a rest. He himself pretended to go to sleep but he had other plans. He quietly went and found out the way by which Monsopiad would return to his home in Kampung Kurai. He then hid behind a big tree with the intention of ambushing Monsopiad. When the latter was on his way home Gantang suddenly aimed a blow at him with his parang from behind but his blow missed. Then Monsopiad counter-attacked and after a hard struggle Gantang was defeated; he died on the spot and his head was cut off. Monsopiad cut up the body; he himself took a leg back to the house of Gantang for the people to see. At first they were very surprised but then they wanted to attack him. However, he escaped from them.

Monsopiad and the seven little boys brought Gantang's head and an arm to Kampung Kurai and that is the bone among the skulls at the house of Dousia. The head of Gantang is also there—one of the forty-two (Moujing, Race).[4]

---

[4]Moujing, Race (pers. comm.) was a student field-worker from Kampung Kandazon, Penampang.

Later during the evening on Tuesday, there was *sumazau* and at 11.00 p.m. there was the special dance performed on such occasions and known as *lumampag*. About 30 persons lined up behind one another, each one putting his hands on the shoulders of the one in front, and to the beating of the gongs, the dancers stamped their feet on the floor. The one in front, whose hands were free, led them in their singing as they danced. The purpose of the *lumampag* is to frighten away spirits of bad luck. And so ended the fourth day of the *Magang*.

Nothing special took place on Wednesday, the fifth day of the *Magang*, until evening. At about 6.00 p.m. there was the drinking of *habot-tapai* which had been specially made and blessed by the *bobohizan* during the *magavau* ceremony which had taken place some weeks earlier. This drinking of the *habot* was reserved for the family as it was only the owner of the house, Dousia and his brothers and sisters and close cousins who were permitted to drink the *habot*. However, other people were present. The *habot* had to be drunk from a cup made from bamboo (*suki*). The custom is that the bamboo cups are not used again but kept in the house until they decay. The night concluded with the dancing of the *sumazau*.

Thursday and Friday, the 6th and 7th days of the *Magang* were not marked by any special functions, except that the festival spirit continued particularly in the line of food and drinks; at night the *sumazau* was again danced. On Thursday three of the *bobohizan* from Kampung Hungab who had been staying in Dousia's house went to perform a *Magang* on a smaller scale at the house of Encik Sikui Molijip at Kampung Puhutan, about half a mile away.

Bianti also went but returned to her own home at night time. The two flags used at Dousia's were taken and hoisted outside Sikui's house. Bianti spent some hours at Sikui's on Friday and Saturday also. The *Magang* at Dousia's came to a conclusion on Friday night with the *sumazau* and the taking down of the gongs.

Some facts about the financial aspect of the *Magang* may help to give a better impression of its magnitude. In all, about five hundred people attended at one time or another. To supply food, there were slaughtered: a two-and-a-half year old male buffalo (approximate value: RM 350.00), three pigs (approximate value: RM 120.00 each), ten chickens (approximate value: RM 6.00 each). About sixty *gantangs* of rice was consumed and the amount of rice used to make *tapai* and *hiing* was seventy *gantangs*. All of this rice would be valued at RM 500.00. Goods that had to be purchased included: fish—RM 30.00, beer and stout—RM 900.00, soft drinks—RM 120.00. No estimate has been made of the amount spent on vegetables, onions, curry powder, cooking oil, etc. Some of those who attended the *Magang* brought gifts and an estimation is as follows: 20% presented tapai, 5% presented beer or stout, 40% presented money gifts, leaving 35% who brought nothing. A leg and shoulder of the buffalo and three *gantangs* of rice was the remuneration given to the *bobohizan*. The overall expenditure was in the region of RM 3000.00.

Dousia and those directly connected with the *Magang* felt satisfied that everything had been done properly and that they had fulfilled their duties to the spirits of the skulls (*bangkavan*) in a very satisfactory manner.

It has been mentioned already that there was another *Magang* in the same locality that partly coincided with the one held in Kampung

Fig. 29. The house of Sikui witrh the *Magang* flags hanging from the windows.

Kandazon. This second *Magang* was observed in the home of Encik Sikui Molijip of Kampung Puhutan, also known as Kampung Koduntut and situated in the larger Kampung Kurai (Fig. 29). The rituals carried out were similar to those already recorded and, therefore, the information given here shall be confined to the background story of this particular *Magang* and any items peculiar to it.

Encik Sikui Molijip is an employee of the Lands and Surveys Department. He owns some land and buffaloes. He married Singkiep in 1956 and they have a large family. He completed the building of a new house in November, 1969.

The mother of Singkiep, his wife, is named Joimi and has been a widow for many years. She has three children, Singkiep the eldest, and two sons. Joimi had one skull in her home; she probably felt that it was time to pass it on to the next generation. It seems that her choice of Singkiep as the recipient was not simply because she was her eldest child—her two sons are Christians and were possibly not interested. Joimi's home is in Kampung Kurai, about one mile from that of her daughter. The previous Magang for this skull was held in 1957, the occasion when Joimi moved into her newly constructed house.

Attached to the bamboo that carried the skull was a large sea-shell, a conch (Fig. 30). The explanation given for this shell involved the whole story of the skull. Long ago a farmer and his wife from Kampung Kurai went to fish in the sea, which from here is a few miles away. The wife was pregnant and after some time fishing, she lay down on the beach to take a rest and fell asleep. While there, someone came and cut off her head. When the husband discovered the headless body of his wife, he returned to his kampung and told the story. A group of men of the village armed themselves and set out to take revenge. They captured a Suluk, whom they believed to have committed the crime, killed him and took home his head. Since the Suluks were associated with the sea, they also brought with them a large sea-shell which has been kept with the skull ever since.

It is difficult to say how authentic the story is. At certain times during the *Magang,* a person blew through the conch and made a loud noise. This same practice is recorded by Evans in a brief description of a

Fig. 30. *Bobohizan* Binjulip preparing new *hisad* for the conch and the skull (held here by Sikui).

head-hunting ceremony held in Tuaran district: 'The leader of the party carried a conch-shell (*tabhuri*) on which he blew occasional blasts,' (1923: 12).

The *Magang* commenced at 7.00 p.m. on the 9th May. On the following day, the skull and the conch were carried from the home of Joimi to that of Sikui with the usual ceremony. Since there were seven pieces of *hisad* tied to the bamboo with the skull, seven new pieces of *hisad* had to be prepared (Fig. 31). The *hisad* had been collected from Kampung Kibabaig near Kasigui, Penampang. Sikui had consulted the chief priestess, Bianti, concerning the most suitable time to hold the *Magang*. He said that the usual time for a *Magang* was in the month of May when all the *Magavau* ceremonies were over.

On the third day of the *Magang* at the house of Sikui a large menhir was visited and honour given to the spirit *Gunsolong* which is believed to reside in it. The visitation was to have taken place at about midday, but because of a heavy shower of rain, it was delayed until about 2.00 p.m. While waiting, many took turns dancing the *sumazau*.

Fig. 31 (above). Three priestesses preparing *hisad*. **Fig. 32** (below). Procession to the menhir named *Gunsolong*.

The procession to the menhir was led by four *bobohizan* accompanied by some other women (Fig. 32). One of the two flags hoisted for a *Magang* was carried along. Sikui walked next to the *bobohizan;* he was wearing a *siga*—the Kadazan head-cloth—and he also had a long ceremonial sword (*padang*) inside a colourful scabbard slung from his left shoulder. Some people brought the *hisad* and the two pieces of white cloth. Two gongs and a drum were beaten along the way. Two men blew through bamboo flutes—*tobuii.* Close behind the *bobohizan,* one man carried the conch that was normally tied to the bamboo beside the skull. Periodically, as the group proceeded, he blew through it.

A large jar of *tapai* suspended from a pole resting on the shoulders of two men was another important item. One of the *bobohizan* sprinkled white rice along the mile-long journey as they walked and chanted. One woman carried some of the blood of the pig that had been slaughtered earlier that morning; it was inside a bamboo container (*hangod*). It was an impressive group, though some were merely curious observers.

The menhir which they visited is nearly ten feet (3 m) tall. It is situated on a bund next to a padi-field owned by Singkiep and the monument is considered to be her property; it is about one mile or slightly more from their home following the road that existed in 1974. According to one story, a girl was passing this stone one day and the spirit in the stone asked her where she was going. She made no reply but simply stood and stared at the stone. The spirit was angry and when the girl reached home, the spirit caused her to become very sick. The illness was so serious that a *bobohizan* was called; she diagnosed the cause of the illness. The family gave the *bobohizan* a chicken to offer to the spirit. After the *bobohizan* had made the offering and chanted some prayers, the girl regained her health. Ever afterwards the stone has been known as *Gunsolong* which means 'the one who stares.'

The rituals that were carried out with regard to the menhir were similar to those held during the *Magang* at the house of Dousia except that the menhir was so high and shaped in such a manner that Sikui was unable to stand on it; he sat on the top of it and poured the pig's blood on the section of the stone in front of him and behind him (Fig. 33). The expenditure on Sikui's family for this *Magang* ceremony was approximately RM 1000.00.

What will become of the skulls owned by Dousia? His children are not interested in them and, in particular, they do not wish to take on the responsibility of carrying out celebrations intended to show respect to the spirits of the skulls. Dousia has stated,

Fig. 33. Encik Sikui pouring blood on a menhir.

> "I told them [my children] *jangan kacau* (don't disturb them). They cannot surrender them to the museum, church or even bury them when I am gone. What they can do if they are sick of seeing the skulls or feel it is in conflict with their new beliefs is to build a separate house and hang them there. After all, the skulls have accepted getting used to the *Monogit* not being held regularly. So the question of feeding them does not arise. It is important to keep passing them down to future generations. The moment anyone in my family tree in future surrenders them, our honour and that of Monsopiad will be no more." (Sarda, 1994: 63).

Another person, Anthony Lojuta of Kampung Hungab, Penampang, is facing a similar problem (Fig. 34 & 35). Anthony has no children and none of his relatives is interested in taking possession of the skulls hanging in his house. According to a report (Sarda, 1994: 6)

> "Anthony's wife, Taliah Jangkat, claims there have been cases of families who had surrendered them without following proper procedures incurring the wrath of the spirits. Unlike burial jars, she says such skulls cannot be surrendered to the church or museum. 'They (family members) may go blind, insane or suffer other forms of hardship in the long term. There must be a final grand feast involving the slaughter of a buffalo and the skulls told politely that

Skulls hanging in the home of Mr. Anthony Lojuta in Kampung Hungab. **Fig. 34** (above) was taken in 1974 and **Fig. 35** (below) was taken in 2000.

TAHAP—MAGANG

GUNDOHING SOIMON LAJANGAN OM SAVO

Agazo oginavo magahap di ....
do tumindapou kalamazan do MAGANG ih kaanjul do 7 tadau hinaid
mantad ko 6-4-1974 gisom ko 12-4-1974
doid hinominon za do Kampung Koidupan, Nosoob

Ahansan do kotindapou kou
do ontok tadau Minggu ko 7-4-1974
do ataandak nodii daa oh kalamazan za
diho nokomoi.

Copy of an invitation card requesting a guest's attendance at a *Magang* Ceremony held in April, 1974

(Translation of the above)

INVITATION—*MAGANG*
Mr. & Mrs. Soimon Lajangan
cordially invite ....
to attend a *Magang* celebration, which will last for 7 consecutive days,
from 6-4-1974 to 12-4-1974
at their Residence at Kampung Koidupan, Nosoob.
Your presence on Sunday, 7-4-1974
will be very much appreciated.

they have to finally leave because there is no one to care for them anymore. All the skulls and bones will then be placed in a single coffin and accorded a normal burial.'"

A third *Magang* that was held in the Penampang District in 1974 was at the home of Soimon Lajangan in Kampung Koidupan, Nosoob. It is of particular interest because priests and priestesses of a different rite—the *Tagaas* rite—were involved. The two former *Magang* ceremonies described above were according to the Kadazan rite.

This *Magang* at the home of Soimon took place from 6th to 12th April, 1974. The purpose of the ceremony was to hold a celebration in honour of the spirits that are believed to reside in a *tinambang*—a wooden figure said to resemble a deer and which has a head, two front legs, a very long body and tail and which is thirteen feet (4 m) from one end to the other (Fig. 36). It is suspended from the ceiling and *hisad is* tied round it just as *hisad* is tied round the bamboo to which skulls are attached. It is said that a forefather of Soimon had about twenty skulls in his home. Accidentally the house was destroyed by fire and the skulls with it. It was later divined by a *bobohizan* that the spirits of the skulls had no longer any place to stay and wanted a place of abode. It was decided to make the *tinambang* for them and since that time the spirits and the *tinambang* have been treated as if the skulls were still there.

Fig. 36. The *tinambang*.

The previous *Magang* for the *tinambang* and its spirits was said to have been held about thirty years previously. The decision to celebrate this *Magang* was arrived at in 1972. Soimon had some dreams and a recurring theme was that his grandfather and grandmother were asking for something; but it would be impossible to understand what they wanted unless a *Magang* was held. Because of necessary preparations and expenditure it was decided to hold the *Magang* in 1974. According to informants at the ceremony, the correct time for commencing a *Magang* is a few days after a new moon. However, according to a Chinese calender the 6th April, 1974 happened to be the 14th day of the third moon. And the first day of the *Magang* at the house of Dousia was the 13th day of the fourth moon.

Early on the morning of Saturday, 6th April, a group of twelve men set out in a landrover to fetch *hisad.* Before leaving, they cut five bamboo flag-poles and made three *tobuii* at a place called *Modupo* which is not far from Soimon's house. Their destination for the collection of the *hisad* was Topoko'on at Mile 29 on the Kota Belud road. When asked why they went so far to get some *hisad,* it was stated that this was the place where they had always obtained the *hisad.* It is difficult to believe that they would venture so far afield during the pre-motorcar era. Among the group were two priests or male *bobohizan* and sometimes known as *tabit.* They were: the chief priest, Lobinjang of Kampung Minintod, and his assistant on this occasion, Jomilus of Kampung Koidupan. The group carried with them the bamboo poles that would act as flag-staffs, five flags, and some *tapai.*

At Topoko'on, Lobinjang chanted certain prayers to the spirits in the *hisad* and explained to them what he and his companions intended to do. On the homeward journey they stopped at Kapayan. At about 3.45 p.m., all of the group except the driver of the landrover set out to walk across the padi-land from Kapayan to Kampung Koidupan (Fig. 37). Five of the men carried varied coloured flags approximately 6 feet by 4 feet (1.8 m by 1.2 m) hoisted on the bamboo flag-poles which were about 15 feet (4.6 m) long (Fig. 38). Tied to the each pole was a *hisad* leaf.

The group visited five stone monuments (menhirs) and four wooden monuments *(sininggazanak)* on their way across the padi-land. When the group was about to begin, they were seen from the Koidupan side and about eight men went to meet them and they joined in at the second monument. At each monument the *bobohizan* chanted prayers and at intervals the rest of the men joined in with a chorus. The prayers were to

Fig. 37 (above). Visiting stone and wooden monuments in the padi fields. **Fig. 38** (below). Flags were carried as part of the procession from Kapayan to Koidupan.

Fig. 39. Chanting prayers at a menhir.

please the spirits in the monuments—one in each. On their way from one monument to the next, the men also chanted and some blew the *tobuii.* The group with the five flags moving across the bare plain was an impressive sight.

The length of time spent at each monument was about six minutes (Fig. 39). After a couple of minutes chanting, the *bobohizan* put a *hisad* leaf standing in the ground at the foot of the menhirs and placed one through a crack or crevice in the wood of the *sininggazanak.*

The *hisad* leaf once placed beside or on a monument became known as *'Pinonogindai'*. Its purpose was to show that the monument had been visited and its spirit been prayed to as part of the *Magang* ceremony. After further prayers, the *bobohizan* poured about a quarter of a pint of *tapai* over the monument (Fig. 40). This was an offering to the spirit of the monument.

One of the wooden monuments in the area is in a locality called *Kodundungan* but not the same as Kampung Kodundungan. The monument has the form of the figure of a woman and is locally called *'sininggazanak tondu'* which means 'Woman Statue'. This

Fig. 40. Pouring rice-wine on a menhir.

sininggazanak was not visited because the group passed by a couple of fields away and the figure, being less than three feet tall, was overlooked. Soon it was realised that it had not been visited but it was then impossible to do so as it would not be religiously proper for the group to go back on its tracks.

Lobinjang, the chief *bobohizan* wore ordinary western style pants and shoes and a batik shirt; in addition he had the traditional Kadazan headcloth (*siga*) and a *solindang*—a cloth worn over one shoulder and across the body, but probably because of the long and tiresome journey Lobinjang did not wear it with a great deal of distinction. He carried a curved ceremonial sword (*padang*) which was about 18 inches (46 cm) long and which was inside a decorated scabbard and he had a *siga* on over his hat.

When the group had visited the monuments, it made its way to the home of Soimon who was holding the *Magang*. It arrived at about 5.30 p.m. Some forty yards from the house, the group stopped and two lady *bobohizan* approached slowly from the home of Soimon. They had no covering on their heads but they were dressed in the long, black Kadazan ceremonial costume. Each wore two *husob*. Both had winnows which were held in both hands and they waved them up and down (Fig. 41). The priestesses moved through the group of men who had come from the padi-fields and when they reached about ten yards to the rear of the group, they turned and they all moved to the house. This little ceremony with the winnows was to frighten away any bad spirits that might have joined the group and to ensure that no evil spirits entered the house. Outside the entrance there was a third lady *bobohizan* who gave all who

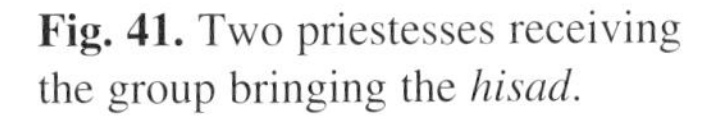

Fig. 41. Two priestesses receiving the group bringing the *hisad*.

entered a generous sprinkling of lustral-water. This water is known as *bokis'*. A *bobohizan* uses the leaves of seven different trees or plants in preparing it: these usually consist of:

Tagandap	—	*Ixora stenophylla* (Family Rubiaceae)
Hisang	—	*Litsea lancifolia* (Family Lauraceae)
Tutumatak	—	*Eugenia* sp.
Dompu	—	*Glochidion obscurum* Hk. *cf Glochidion superbus* Baill.
Boibi	—	*Pandanus* sp. (Family Pandanaceae)
Guo	—	*Colocasia antiquorum* (Family Araceae)
Tongkuango	—	*Ixora coccinea* (Family Rubiaceae)

It is permissible to use *tuka—Dendrobium aloifolium* (Family Orchidaceae)—instead of *boibi* and to use *kuhupak* (bract of banana's inflorescence) instead of *guo.* The lustral water is sprinkled by using leaves. (This practice occurs on other occasions also as at a wedding.) The purpose here was said to have been to give a blessing to those people who had gone praying to the spirits in the monuments. The sprinkling with lustral water and its use for ceremonial cleansing is recognised as an ancient practice in various cultures. In the Bible we read: 'Then I shall sprinkle pure water over you and you shall be made clean—cleansed from the defilement of all your idols' (Ezekiel, 36: 25).

This symbolic cleansing with water applied not only to people but to objects also:

> 'Eleazar the priest said to the soldiers who had come back from the campaign, 'This is a statute of the Law which Yahweh has commanded Moses. Whereas the gold, silver, bronze, iron, tin and lead, everything that can withstand fire, must be passed through the fire and it will be clean, yet it must still be purified with lustral water.' (Numbers, 31: 21–23).

One bamboo flagpole with the flag still attached was tied to a small archway in an upright position about ten feet from the entrance to the house of Soimon. The other four flags were taken inside the house and the flagpoles were fixed horizontally about one foot below the ceiling of the living room and the flags remained suspended from them. The living room was on the ground floor. The flag outside was left flying day and night until the end of the *Magang*. Its purpose was to show that a *Magang* was being held. Any coloured or multi-coloured cloth could be used as a flag but white material would not be permissible.

In the living room, there was new linoleum on the floor. The *bobohizan* and their assistants took their places in a section of the room where there was a new rush mat. A meal of rice and fish in various forms including fish curry was then served to all. *Tapai, hiing,* beer and stout were also served. Very conspicuous in the centre of the room beside a pillar were two jars of *tapai* with drinking reeds in each.

After about forty minutes the next stage of the ceremony commenced. The three lady *bobohizan* sat on the floor with the *hisad* leaves that had been brought from Topoko'on standing against the wall behind them. About five other women sat beside the *bobohizan.* Opposite and approximately eight feet away sat *bobohizan* Lobinjang (Fig. 42). He was surrounded by seven or eight men. After some preliminary chanting, the chief lady *bobohizan* questioned Lobinjang about where he had been,

Fig. 42. The choral dialogue between the priest and the priestesses.

what he had seen and done. Questions and answers were chanted or sung and at the end of each answer, there was a chorus in which all joined. The *tobuii* were also blown periodically.

The question and answer session lasted about one hour and when it was over, there followed a special dance performed by two of the lady *bobohizan* and was more ceremonial than the normal (Fig. 43). Dancing continued into the small hours of the morning, and so ended the first day of the *Magang*.

Fig. 43. A ritual dance by two priestesses.

At about 9.00 a.m. on the morning of Sunday, a buffalo was slaughtered. Many were engaged throughout the forenoon in preparing for the main meal which would be at midday. Many invited guests arrived, some coming from as far away as Sandakan and Brunei. Because of the large number present the serving of lunch lasted a couple of hours. Around 2.30 p.m. one of the highlights of the *Magang* took place—the *tinambang* was lowered from its usual place next to the ceiling and it was "allowed to dance": with the *tinambang* resting on their shoulders, four men (including Soimon) performed a dance. Later the *tinambang* was placed on two upturned *tadang* in the living room on the ground floor.

Then those present danced the *sumazau* and gradually during the late afternoon some of the guests left, but many stayed on for the evening meal and further dancing.

Nothing special took place on Monday and Tuesday. The *bobohizan* spent long periods preparing the *hisad* which would be attached to the *tinambang*. According to the custom of this group, nothing should be killed on the third day of the *Magang*. The festive spirit continued and each evening and night there was *sumazau*.

On Wednesday, the *tinambang* was "allowed to dance" again. By now it had been decorated to the satisfaction of all concerned with fresh *hisad*. With due ceremony it was returned to its place near the ceiling. The flag-poles and the *tobuii* were tied beside it (Fig. 44).

On Thursday, all of the *bobohizan* returned to their homes but came back the next and final day, Friday, to bring the ceremony to an end. After a final *sumazau* in the afternoon, the gongs (*tagung*) were lowered and the *Magang* was over.

Fig. 44. The *tinambang* back in its normal place.

The family of Soimon estimated that about one thousand people visited them during the *Magang*. Five hundred printed invitation cards were sent out but those from nearby kampungs were invited orally. The expenditure totalled about RM 3000.00. Thirty jars of alcohol were made and each jar contained 2.5 gallons, that is, 75 gallons altogether. According to the *Tagaas* rite, which was followed here, no pigs or chickens are killed for a *Magang*; consequently, the amount spent on fish was quite high—about RM 400.00. Approximately RM 600.00 were spent on beer and stout and RM 200.00 on soft drinks.

It was estimated that of all those who came to the *Magang,* about 30% brought gifts of *tapai* or *montoku*, 10% gave presents of money and that 60% brought nothing. The recompense for the *bobohizan* was five dollars each and the hind-quarters of the slaughtered buffalo were divided among them.

An interesting sequel to the *Magang* was a letter written by Lobinjang, the priest, to Soimon a few days after the *Magang*. The two priestesses, Jinggunis and Pinggulin, were due to officiate at a *Monogit* Ceremony at Soimon's house two weeks after the *Magang* and Lobinjang had some requests to make: Herewith the letter, with some amplification provided within brackets:

> 'Soimon,
>
> My thanks to both of you (husband and wife). Please do not be surprised or unduly worried on receiving this letter. All I want to tell the two of you is this that at the end of the celebration (the *magang)* I was not at my best. Perhaps I was giddy due to the presence of a large crowd or probably I over-ate. Nevertheless, I am sure that I was not that drunk (from over-drinking of alcohol). It is true I ate well. Anyhow I was in such a bad state then that I was barely conscious.
>
> Actually the proper thing to have been done (in ending the ceremony) was to have performed the final rite (a chant like a final hymn) of bidding farewell to all the guardian spirits present—to wish them well (for the good of everyone). That is how it should have been—the way our ancestors had always

done it. It was then my fault (that things were not properly done). Anyway, I hope you will not take this too much to heart, and please convey my apology to Pinggulin and especially to Jinggunis (two assisting priestesses at the ceremony). This is what I would like them to know so that when the next part of the celebration comes, they should make it a point to make some sacrificial offerings to the heavens (the abode of good spirits and the guardian spirits). The name of the particular spirits, *tasab* (to whom the offerings are to be made) cannot be mentioned (forbidden by custom) because this particular group of spirits is the keeper or guardian of the ancient promise or covenant.

(Now follows what seems to be part of a dream but it is not explained).

The spirit said:

'We were puzzled; what could these noises and sounds of merriment be down below, sounds like the fulfillment of the covenant (or the carrying out of the promises or agreement made between heaven and men). Then we went down to have a look. When we arrived, the promise had been fulfilled. When we approached the chief of the guardian spirits, we found that the ritual had been correctly performed, as had always been done formerly. But then we were asked who we were. We did not answer for we had reason to be ashamed (had not been invited to come) and might be mistaken for the devils (evil spirits). Anyway we explained our presence—we heard the chantings (of the priest and priestesses) and it attracted us. This is what we came to find out about. However, we would have liked to join in the singing (chanting) before we were sent off. Anyway in the old days everyone (everyone invited to it) was present for this ceremony of the fulfilling of the promises. In this case we came as mere visitors.'

So said the spirits from heaven.

This is what had happened; the heavenly spirits had not been invited. Anyhow who would ever think of inviting these other

> spirits? It is not easy to understand them or their behaviour. They do not think or behave in the same way as we humans do.
>
> So Pinggulin and Jinggunis, when you begin the next part of the ceremony (i.e., *momohumpatiu*) do not forget to go and placate and give peace offerings to them, but don't overdo it because they may take it as their rights. But don't ignore them either or they may take offence and so may cause troubles.
>
> How I came to know of this is that almost every night I have this (dream?)..."

It is unfortunate that the final part of the letter on the third page was misplaced and lost.

In November, 1991 I returned to Kampong Koidupan with the intention of taking better quality photos of the *tinambang* in the home of Mr. Soimon Lajangan. I discovered that Soimon had passed away in 1989. I also learned that about six years after the celebrations of the *Magang* ceremony (that is, about 1980), Soimon became a Christian; at that time the *tinambang* was removed from his home and burned.

Without the actual words of the prayers said by the *bobohizan* during the *Magang* Ceremony, this study is incomplete. However some observations may be made: there is possibly some truth in each of the reasons given in the past for head-hunting, but many of these (such as proof of bravery, the recognition of a youth's entry to manhood, or in order to impress a prospective bride) were probably secondary accretions to a custom that had its origin in religious beliefs associated with a spirit dwelling in each captured skull. The respect with which these skulls are preserved, the celebrations held in their honour and the fear of doing anything that might offend the spirits in the skulls all indicate the belief in a spiritual relationship between the skulls and their owners. The various details in these ceremonies suggest that the most important motivation in head-hunting was connected with religious beliefs. The possessing of one or more skulls was more important than the more adventurous practice of 'hunting' for heads.

Furthermore, it must be noted that what is considered by some to have been a universal practice must have been but a rare event. If all of the suggested types of head-hunting were indulged in continuously over any length of time, and if all the recorded purposes of head-hunting were fulfilled, we should expect to find a large number of skulls and drastic depopulation. However, the number of skulls is relatively very small. It was practically unknown for a man not to marry and if each prospective groom had to take a head in order to win a bride, consider the effects on population. Reference to head-hunting, because of its sensational value, is something that has appealed to scribes of all kinds in the past. The local people had little to report about themselves and their history, but narration of head-hunting stories aroused so much interest that they felt encouraged to stress this practice. The net result for the general public has been the involuntary acquisition of a vague, exaggerated impression about head-hunting.

The era of collecting human skulls through warfare has long come to an end. The survival of inherited skulls that were believed to possess guardian spirits that gave protection and favours to their owners is in jeopardy. And the reason for this is that the spiritual beliefs that sustained this custom have almost vanished.

Chapter 4

HEAD-HOUSES IN TAMBUNAN DISTRICT

In the Tambunan District, the skulls acquired during the period when head-hunting was in vogue are no longer kept and displayed in individual homes. Up to the 1950s, ceremonies were periodically held to honour the spirits of the skulls. There were various reasons why the people of several villages decided to discontinue the traditional custom. The expense of holding a ceremony was high. The beliefs of the people were changing as more and more became Christians. The number of *bobolian* (priests and priestesses of the old animistic system) was declining. Mental attitudes were changing as a result of growing modernization. To free themselves from further obligation to the spirits of the skulls, several villages decided to place the skulls in closed concrete repositories that were constructed near burial grounds or away from dwellings of the villagers.

The House of Skulls at Kampung Sunsuron

(An account based mainly on information provided by Paul Galimbang[5])

The background history to the skull-house at Kampung Sunsuron relates that long ago, relations between the people of Kampung Sunsuron and the inhabitants of some villages on the plain, including in particular Kampung Kituntul, Kampung Tibabar and Kampung

---

[5]Paul Galimbang (pers. comm.) was a student field-worker in Kampung Sunsuron, Tambunan.

Lumandau, grew tense. This tension arose because of thefts that occurred from time to time. Buffaloes disappeared and bamboo fish traps set in the river were missing when the owner went to check his catch.

Complaints from one side led to counter complaints from the other side. Complaints developed into accusations, and in time verbal contention developed into physical warfare. The usual weapon used in such battles was a long sword. In the battles which took place, a warrior who overcome his adversary cut off the victim's head and took it back to his village. Such a head was a demonstration to his kinsfolk of bravery and skill in battle. The warriors collected and stored as many heads as possible.

This situation, which existed in the 19th century, grew much worse with the arrival of Mat Salleh in the Tambunan District. Sporadic fighting had taken place in various parts of Sabah between the forces of the British North Borneo Chartered Company and Mat Salleh and his followers in the years following 1895. In 1898, a treaty was agreed to by Cowie, the Managing Director of the British North Borneo Chartered Company, and Mat Salleh.

The event is related by the historian Tregonning (1965: 203) thus:

> 'Cowie promised Salleh a complete pardon for himself and all his followers. He was told he could have the Tambunan valley in the interior, and that the government would delegate its authority over the people there to him, and would not trouble him. This was extremely generous of Cowie, for the Chartered Company had penetrated into the remote valley only twice, for a fleeting moment, and had never exercised any authority there at all. Only Witti, the early explorer in this unauthorized trek, and later a roaming District Officer had passed through, both very quickly to save their lives from the Dusuns. The occasional message from the Dusuns always stated in an unequivocal manner that if the government left them alone they would do likewise; but if

> invaded they would resist. That remained the position in 1898. This valley and these people were now offered to Salleh. He accepted,...'

Later in his "History of Modern Sabah" Tregonning continues:

> 'In the Tambunan valley Mat Salleh was the focus of attraction of all the bad hats in the country. With forced labour he began building another fort, more powerful than that previously at Ranau. He lived with his followers among the Tagaas Dusun, at the upper end of the valley, and soon began raiding and molesting the Tambunan Dusuns in the south. With Salleh breaking their old jars and taking their rice their dislike for the European abated, and in early 1899 they asked Fraser, the nearest District Officer at Keningau to protect them.' (op. cit.: 205).

The memory of the Mat Salleh era in Tambunan survives in the oral tradition of the people. Those whose sympathy leaned towards Sunsuron stated that the inhabitants there felt very worried when Mat Salleh took up residence with their traditional enemies. These latter incited Mat Salleh to oppress the people of Sunsuron. He demanded the payment of chickens and pigs as a form of tax and Sunsuron paid. On two occasions Mat Salleh asked Sunsuron to give buffaloes and the animals were supplied. But Mat Salleh was not satisfied and, according to a present-day elderly resident, felt that he should receive more honour from the people of Sunsuron. He asked that two rich men (Simbayon and Gadog) surrender themselves to him. This demand was refused and with the refusal, Mat Salleh was informed that it was obvious that his purpose was to oppress and humiliate the people of Sunsuron. This reply caused Mat Salleh to become very angry and he made attacks on them. Since they were outnumbered, they sent a representative to obtain help from the British in Labuan.

Four Europeans, two Indians and a force consisting mainly of Dayaks later arrived with weapons of war. With the help of the people of Sunsuron they defeated Mat Salleh in 1900.

During this war, the fighting men of Sunsuron collected heads of enemies killed in battle. After peace was restored, all the skulls that had been obtained were kept in a house specially made for storing them. The house was made of wood and bamboo. People of Kampung Karanaan and Kampung Nambayan, who assisted Kampung Sunsuron in the fighting, also took heads and kept them in a special place in their respective villages.

The wooden head-house in Kampung Sunsuron was replaced several times, because the materials did not last. The people were not happy about the necessity to replace the building from time to time and they decided to build a concrete structure for the purpose of housing the skulls.

The 'head-house' was erected near a burial ground and separated from the village by a ravine. According to inscriptions on the concrete that are still legible, the structure was erected in June, 1959. The name of the builder is given as Y.N. Gampin.

The plan of the head-house is almost square: the width of the front and back is 38.5 inches (0.98 m) and the two sides are 33.5 inches (0.85 m) (Fig. 45). The four walls are 47 inches (1.19 m) high and the roof is in the form of a pyramid. The apex of the pyramid is surmounted with a concrete image of a skull which is 22 inches (59 cm) in circumference. There is no door in the 'head-house' but there is a window in the front measuring 11 inches by 9 inches (28 cm by 23 cm), and there is a two inch (5 cm) overhang above the window to prevent rain from going inside. Through the window skulls can be seen inside and there is wire in the window to prevent the removal of any of them.

Thomas R. Williams, an American anthropologist, lived in Kampung Sunsuron from August, 1959 to August, 1960. In his book "The Dusun", based on research he carried out in Kampung Sunsuron, he does not refer to the concrete 'head-house' but he has this to say about the aftermath of a successful head-hunting raid:

'On return to their village the raiding party usually hangs head and hand trophies, wrapped in leaf and rattan covers, on the lower branches of a special tree near the village area. Here they are greeted by female specialists playing songs of victory upon a bamboo war flute, and by gong and drum music. Head and hand trophies are allowed to remain on the tree at least long enough for the flesh to rot away and then are put into a special trophy house until the triennial ritual of Menebi, celebrating past wrongs being righted through victory in war... The trophy structure, most often a small square platform raised on wooden posts, and roofed and sided with bamboo, is at a central location in the community. There it serves the purpose of a *tinaleg,* or symbol of "sacredness", and as reminder of the bravery of village warriors in avenging offenses against traditional law.' (Williams, 1965: 67).

Fig. 45. The head-house at Kampung Sunsuron.

The first person who was in charge of the concrete 'head-house' and its contents was Ompin or the Y.N. Gampin whose name is inscribed on the monument. After his death he was succeeded by Gotowik. This man now lives in Kampung Mogong but was originally from Kampung Sunsuron. He is a male *bobolian* (priest in the animistic form of religion of the Dusun/Kadazan people).

Writing in 1970 Whelan referred to the skulls at Kampung Sunsuron and stated:

> 'At present there is a head-house in Sunsuron village on the Tambunan plain. If you want to see it you must ask the head-house keeper to take you. If you go alone you must pay two dollars *sogit* to the village.' (Whelan 1970: 40).

According to the belief of some of the elderly people of Kampung Sunsuron, the skulls are endowed with supernatural power by which they can affect anyone who disturbs them. If a person steals a skull, the spirit in the skull will cause him to die or to become insane. Two examples are quoted: (*a*) A man, who shall be known as X, took a skull from the 'head-house' and sold it to the museum. Not long afterwards the wife of X died and a few months later, X himself passed away. (*b*) Another man took a skull just for the fun of doing so. It was said that as a result of his disrespect he became mentally ill.

However, it is possible to obtain and take away a skull from the 'head- house' if proper *adat* is observed. First of all it is necessary to contact Gotowik, the custodian of the skulls, and make known one's wish to him. If he approves, it will be necessary to make a payment. Before the skull can be removed Gotowik must communicate with the spirit that in residing in the skull and request the spirit not to cause any harm to the person who intends to take it. The skull is bathed in lustral water and a fowl is slaughtered in offering to the spirit in the skull. In this way, the new owner of the skull will be safe from any harm.

Williams (1965: 67) made a study of the skulls in the 'head-house' in Kampung Sunsuron and here are given his findings and conclusions:

> 'Age and sex determination of some 35 skull trophies present in 1959–1960 in the Sunsuron trophy house gave an indication that much recent head-hunting warfare was directed against the aged, adolescents, and females; at least half the skulls were female, the majority being either young or very old, while some 10 percent of the remainder were adolescent boys.'

In an account written by a student in 1970 about "The Skulls of Sinsuron" it was stated that the acquisition of the skulls resulted from successful raids against the Tibabars. At first the skulls were of great benefit to their keepers:

> 'It is said that whenever their enemies approached their village, these skulls would shout to warn the people' (Pius Kating, 1989: 51).

Later in the same account, it was described how the Sinsurons made an all-out attempt to wipe out the Tibabars. Their attack was successful but an anti-climax seems to have followed:

> 'But despite their victory, it was believed that the skulls were slowly destroying the Sinsurons. Several warriors died from all kinds of sickness which nobody could explain. In the end, the skulls were left to rot all over the place. Today if one visits Kampong Sinsuron in the Tambunan District, one can still see some of these skulls.' (op. cit.: 51).

The House of Skulls in Kampung Karanaan

(An account based mainly on information provided by Mathilda Taliban[6])

The 'head-house' at Kampung Karanaan is less well-known than that in Kampung Sunsuron. This lack of notoriety is due to two or three factors:

---

[6]Mathilda Taliban (pers. comm.) is a teacher and also an assistant researcher in Kampung Karanaan Tambunan.

a) it is located in a position which is not readily noticeable;
b) the number of skulls preserved there is much smaller;
c) the skulls were the property of one family and not of the village until 1972.

The 'head-house' is situated at the edge of a small burial ground. The monument is about one hundred yards from the main road and it is necessary to pass through a field in order to enter the burial ground where the 'head-house' is located. Some bamboo vegetation growing on the boundary of the area overhangs the 'head-house'.

The monument at Kampung Karanaan is similar in size to that at Kampung Sunsuron. It was erected in 1972 according to the inscription it bears and the people responsible for building it probably modelled the structure on that at Kampung Sunsuron. The main difference in its form is that the roof consists of a flat concrete slab. At the present time the roof is not covering the structure but leaning against the side of it. It seems that buffaloes rubbed against it and knocked the roof off (Fig. 46).

Fig. 46. The head-house at Kampung Karanaan.

There is no special name for this 'head-house' but it is variously known as *Bangkavan* or *Guritum* (skull) or by the Malay term *Rumah Tengkorak.* The floor is covered with decaying leaves which fall from the overhanging trees. However, it is possible to see inside, among the leaves, four human skulls and a wooden image of a skull. The people to whom the skulls belonged in life are said to have been Muruts who lived in the area around Rundum in the Tenom District. The heads were those of men and the explanation for the wooden image is the fact that the raiding party did not have time to take the head of one man who had been killed. It is surprising to hear that a head-hunting party ranged so far afield, the distance between Tambunan and Rundum being about 90 miles (150 km). However, one of the heads was taken from the Toboh area of the Tambunan plain and, consequently, was probably that of a Dusun.

It is believed by some of the local people that there is a spirit in each of the skulls and also in the wooden image, and that these spirits are those of the individuals who were killed. The spirits are considered to have so much power because they have been fed ever since they were taken. They are considered good or bad spirits according to the manner in which they are looked after; if well cared for, they are favourable but if offerings are not made to them, they may bring misfortune.

Previous to 1972, the skulls were kept in the home of Muja who is still residing in Kampung Karanaan. The probable reason for keeping all the skulls there was because it was the grandfather of Muja, a man named Samadal, who took the heads from the Toboh area. Each year it was necessary to hold a ceremonial feast to honour the spirits in the skulls. Some say that there was no special name for the ceremony and there was no fixed time in the year for holding it. Though the people of the village donated money, rice, chickens and *tapai* for the ceremony, the ultimate responsibility and burden lay on Muja or his father or grandfather.

The suggestions of housing the skulls in a special building away from the village came from the family of Muja. This was in imitation of what had been done at Kampung Sunsuron, but probably the principal consideration was the fact that it would no longer be necessary to make annual offerings to and hold celebrations for the spirits of the skulls.

However, the transfer of the skulls was an elaborate event. The ceremony and festivities that accompanied it lasted three days. Three *bobolian* (one man and two women) officiated. The expenses involved are estimated to have been in the region of RM 3000. About one-quarter of the amount was contributed by the people of the village and the remainder was provided by Muja's family.

The house for the skulls was built by the residents of Kampung Karanaan and the cost was met by donations from the people, though Muja's family provided more than any other. The site chosen was in a quiet place, remote from the activities of the village so that there would be little likelihood of the skulls being disturbed.

The structure has the following dimensions: Length: 48 inches; width: 33 inches; height: 36 inches. On the front above a small window is written: *"TENGKORAK 1900-1972"*. (SKULLS 1900–1972). On either side of the window and slightly below it are the drawings of two skulls. Close to the bottom and beneath the window is the single English word "HUMAN". On the side of the structure is an inscription in Malay:

(Actual Inscription)

TUGU PERINGATAN TENGKORAK
Kepala Telah Di-ambil Pada 1890
Dipindahkan di Tempat ini pada 15–4–72

(Translation)

MONUMENT IN MEMORY OF SKULLS
The Heads were taken in 1890
Transferred to this place on 15–4–72

The possibility of the skulls being interfered with is a constant source of concern for Muja because annoyance to the spirits will be avenged on Muja, or on his family, or on his property such as his livestock. Not long after the transfer of the skulls, Muja lost his eyesight. He had himself immediately taken to a *bobolian* (priestess) to seek help. The diagnosis was that the affliction was a punishment from the spirits because of disturbance caused to them. A ceremony was held during which an offering of a chicken was made to the spirits; later his sight was restored. Muja did not seek the help of modern medicine. The payment to the priestess was two tins of rice and 20 cents. It was surmised that the disturbance to the skulls was caused by children who wandered into this area and poked a stick through the window. Disturbance to the skulls caused by birds or animals will not anger the spirits and no misfortune will result. Other people in the village cannot be harmed as a result of annoyance to the spirits in the skulls: only those individuals living in the house where the skulls were formerly kept can be adversely affected by the wrath of the spirits. Consequently, Muja demands that anyone who approaches the skulls should have his permission or that of the *Ketua Kampung* (Village Chief) of Kampung Karanaan. In the first half of 1980, the left leg of Muja was amputated from below the knee. He was suffering from chronic ulcers. Muja says that the ailment began one day after he had been repairing a fence in an area adjoining the burial ground where the 'head-house' is located.

The House of Skulls at Kampung Kituntul

(An account based mainly on information provided by Robert Gasida[7] and Beatrice M. Podtung[8])

According to oral tradition, the people of Kampung Kituntul originated from Tuaran District and the ancestors migrated to Tambunan area long, long ago. Their first settlement was a village named Kampung Kinoduaan. This village was situated near

[7]Robert Gasida (pers. comm.) was a student field-worker in the villages of the Toboh Plain, Tambunan. [8]Beatrice M. Podtung (pers. comm.) was a student field-worker in the villages of the Toboh Plain, Tambunan.

Kampung Sunsuron. Problems arose between the people of the two villages. The principal difference of opinion was related to the supply of running water for irrigating padi-fields. The problem became so great that it led to warfare and several neighbouring villages took sides; among those that sided with Kampung Kituntul were Kampung Toboh, Kampung Minodung, Kampung Gagaraon and Kampung Sukong. At this period, a renowned warrior in Kampung Kituntul was Gouh and in Kampung Sukong was Banta.

In the battles which ensued, heads were taken and afterwards ceremonies were held to honour the spirits of the skulls. For the celebration in Kampung Kituntul, two buffaloes were slaughtered and the function had the purpose of asking for an increase in fighting ability and for approval to go to war again.

When Mat Salleh came to settle in Tambunan he took the side of Kampung Kituntul and its allies and this group became known as Tagahas. Based on the dialect spoken the following villages: Kampung Karanaan, Kampung Noudu, Kampung Tinompok, Kampung Timbou and Kampung Botung formed an alliance and supported Kampung Sunsuron. With the death of Mat Salleh in 1900, the Chartered Company took control and inter-village fighting ceased.

Though peace was established, a feeling of mistrust lingered on for a long time. Even at the present time if a boy from Kampung Noudu marries a girl from Kampung Toboh, *sogit* may be required: this is an offering to ‘cool’ any tension that might exist from the animosities of the past. Because of the *sogit* the couple living together will not hurt the feelings of the inhabitants of either village. It is a sign that the old quarrel or misunderstanding is forgotten and that they can be friends. At first the *sogit* offering was a buffalo; later it was reduced to a pig, and nowadays, some dispense with the custom altogether.

It is not clear how many collections of skulls were kept by the Tagahas group; but it is certain that some heads were preserved in Kampung Toboh and looked after by a famous priestess named

Timuk, assisted by several other priestesses. After Timuk and some of her companions became Christians, no one was willing to look after the skulls. As a result, a priestess from Kampung Minodung brought them to her village and took responsibility for them. The skulls were placed in a small hut built by the side of a stream. Some children occasionally threw stones at the hut and possibly some of the skulls were thrown out and carried away by floodwaters in time of heavy rain. When the priestess in Kampung Minodung who was in charge of the skulls died, the other priestess was not willing to be responsible for the hut and its contents. The result was that the skulls were moved once more, this time to Kampung Kituntul.

The skulls were welcomed to Kampung Kituntul and during a fitting ceremony held to honour them they were stored in a place called a *Kaiam*.[9] After some time and again with due celebration, the skulls were housed in a rice hut (*sulap*) where they were hung on the inside of the walls.

However, in the present 'head-house' in Kampung Kituntul there are some skulls that were taken in Tenom area, 50 to 60 miles to the south. Two leaders who opposed the British in that region were Gantanom and Balayong. All attempts to capture or kill them failed and it was believed by the people that they possessed a charm which protected their bodies from being pierced by a bullet. The British sought help from Tambunan and among those who offered them assistance were two warriors from Kampung Kituntul named Rumantai and Gimpor. In the warfare which ensued, Gantanom of Tenom was slain by Gimpor. Balayong also met his end and the heads of the two Tenom warriors were taken to Tambunan and at first kept in the house of Rumantai in Kampung Kituntul.

The arrival of the two heads was greeted with celebrations; a buffalo was slaughtered and there was plenty of *tapai* to drink. The purpose of the ceremony was to honour the skulls so that they would guard the people of the village from all sickness and from evil spirits. Later the skulls were transferred to a 'house' specially built for them.

---

[9] In the dialect of Kampung Kituntul *Kaiam* is a word used for skull.

In 1971, it was proposed by a priestess in the village that the two groups of skulls should be kept together in one place. As a result, a concrete repository was constructed, and on 1st November 1971, a ceremony-cum-celebration was held to unite the two groups of skulls and to install them in their new resting place (Fig. 47). On that occasion the majority of the old people participated in the rites. Holding swords in their hands they jumped and danced round the skulls and at the same time gave vent to war cries while the priestesses officiated at the transferring of the skulls to their new home. Those mainly responsible for the new structure were K.K. Sogunting and Mosida.

The repository has the following dimensions: length: 53 inches (1.35 m); width: 47 inches (1.19 m); height: 34 inches (0.86 m). The structure looks very solid though the workmanship lacks the finish expected of craftsmen. The repository consists of two compartments. Embedded in a line across the concrete roof are seven stones; these mark the division between the two compartments and also indicate that there are seven skulls inside. There are two circular openings about three inches in diameter in the sides of each compartment. It is

Fig. 47. The head-house at Kampung Kituntul.

impossible to remove any of the skulls from inside as these apertures are so small; their purpose seems to be for ventilation. The skulls were placed in earthenware jars inside the 'head-house' when it was being constructed. Though it is quite dark inside, it is possible to see at least one jar.

Some people say that the skulls can be frightening at times. It is said that people who live near the 'head-house' in Kampung Sunsuron and Kampung Kituntul can hear all sorts of noises which reflect the ways of life, habits and customs of the people who were contemporaries with the owners of the heads. Singing, crying, screaming and even the playing of the *sompoton* (bamboo mouth organ) can be heard occasionally, especially at night time.

The House of Skulls at Kampung Tibabar

The place where skulls are kept at Kampung Tibabar is a concrete, cube-shaped structure which has the following external dimensions:

Height: 42–45 inches (1.07–1.14 m)
Length: 55 inches (1.4 m)
Breadth: 48 inches (1.2 m)

Fig. 48. The head-house at Kampung Tibabar.

There are no means of opening it; there is a rectangular aperture in the south wall. This aperture measures 10 inches (25.4 cm.) by 9 inches (22.9 cm.) and is 11 inches (28 cm.) from the top of the monument (Fig. 48).

It is possible to decipher writing on the concrete roof of the skull-house. The writing is in four parts and in order to read it one must stand alternately at each of the four sides of the house.

The inscription on the west side:	(Translation)
Pada 25-6-1966 *Rumah Bangkawang disiap* *jam pukul dua 25 minit* *26-6-1966*	(On 26th June, 1966 The House of Skulls was completed at 2.25 p.m. 26th June, 1966)
The inscription on the east side:	(Translation)
Pada 26-6-1966 *Peringatan* *Pasal Belanja untuk buat ini* *Duit dipakai sebanyak* *RM235/– dan seekor kerbau*	(On 26th June, 1966 Remembrance Cost expended to do this Amount of money used RM235/– and a buffalo)
The inscription on the south side:	(Translation)
Pada 26-6-1966 *Peringatan* *Pasal dun' ini dalam tangan* *RM137/– Padtung*	(On 26th June, 1966 Remembrance Amount of money in hand RM137/– Padtung)
The inscription on the north side:	(Translation)
Piniyanaan do Tongkurak *do guhu-guhu om isai-isai* *nopoh tuhun do osodu* *moi intong dih om mositi*	(Place of the skulls which have been handed down from ancient times. Anybody who visits this

manahak do usin gisom kosukaan sondii	place is required to make a donation—the amount is left to the wish of the individual)

In 1991, the person whose name appears on the house of skulls, namely Padtung, was interviewed. He could not remember the exact number of skulls placed in the repository, but he thought that there were at least ten. He said that the reason for constructing this structure for the skulls was that people in the village no longer had the traditional expertise to honour the skulls in the customary manner. He added that nobody paid any attention any longer to the collection of donations: the people were not interested in the house of skulls any more because now most of the inhabitants of the village had become Christians.

It is possible to find some incongruities in the foregoing accounts of the four 'head-house but these discrepancies are of a minor nature. In a rural society where village rivalry was once strong, it is natural to expect some bias in an individual's report of his own village. However, collectively the accounts should help us to understand more fully the minds of those who practiced head-hunting and head-collecting.

ACKNOWLEDGEMENTS

Attempts on my part to persuade senior students to put in writing records of important events in their local culture did not meet with much success. This led to the decision to try "to influence them by example".

Much of the material in this monograph was first published in the Journal of the Sabah Branch of the Malaysian Historical Society (1983). Because of some further research, it has been decided to rewrite the article with some revisions and additions. My thanks are due to the Sabah Branch of the Malaysian Historical Society for permission to publish most of the material in the original article.

Information about many traditional beliefs and customs is fading fast in this age of rapid change to new forms of modern culture. It is hoped that this account of the *Magang* ceremony will bring about a greater awareness of traditional practices and will lead more competent and local commentators to record many other traditional ceremonies and beliefs before such valuable information is lost to posterity.

For assistance in obtaining information about the *Magang* ceremony, thanks are due to the families of Dousia, Soimon and Sikui, and for translation work to Brother Justin Mobilik.

My sincere thanks to Ms. Stella Moo-Tan and Ms. Su Chin Sidih of the Sabah Museum and to Ms. Rita Lasimbang for their valuable assistance and patience in type-formating and other technical comments in the preparation of this work for publication.

The proposal of a revised edition of this book came from Mr. Chan Chew Lun. For this he has worked tirelessly and I sincerely thank him for his dedication in overseeing all the aspects of producing this revised edition.

GLOSSARY

The meanings of some local words that occur in the text:

Adat	Traditional practice or customary law.
Bobolian	A priest or priestess in the Dusun/Kadazan traditional form of religion or a traditional ritual specialist.
Bobohizan	This is another name for *bobolian.*
Hiing	Strong alcoholic drink made from rice; it is also known as *lihing.*
Hisad	A type of palm (*Licuala* sp.) that grows in swampy areas. When the leaf dries, it becomes whitish yellow in colour. It does not disintegrate and retains its appearance for many years. In some areas, it is known as *silad.*
Husap	A small wooden structure or hut built away from one's dwelling. Its purpose may be for use as a temporary place to rest and sleep or as a permanent store for rice-grain. In some areas, it is known as a *sulap.*
Husob	A colourful cloth worn over one shoulder and usually joined or fastened at waist-level on the opposite side of the body; it is known in Malay as *solindang.*
Lihing	This is another name for *hiing.*
Magang	A ceremony usually lasting seven days to honour spirits that are believed to reside in the skulls taken in head-hunting raids.

Mingku'ung	A Dusun/Kadazan dance.
Monogindai	A religious ceremony in the traditional Dusun/Kadazan form of religion.
Pangkis	A cheer used by a leader in a *sumazau* dance; this cheer or shout was the battle-cry of Dusun/Kadazan in olden days when they made an attack on an enemy.
Sindavang	Small cymbals used by priestesses while chanting prayers.
Silad	Another name for *hisad.*
Sininggazanak	A wooden monument erected on the land of a person who had died without leaving a child to inherit his or her land.
Sulap	Another name for *husap*.
Sumazau	A popular Dusun/Kadazan dance.
Tadang	A cylindrically shaped basket strapped on one's back and used for carrying objects or material.
Tapai	An alcoholic drink made from rice or from tapioca.
Tobuii	A type of simple flute made specially for a *magang* ceremony and constructed from bamboo.
Vatu	A stone. *Vatu is* a word used for stone menhirs.

REFERENCES

Borneo Bulletin (1973). The Borneo Bulletin. Kuala Belait, Brunei Darussalam. 29 December, p. 10.

Burbidge, F.W. (1880). *The Gardens of the Sun.* John Muray, London.

Daily Express (1992). "Snippets". Daily Express. Kota Kinabalu, Sabah. 2 February, p. 2.

Domalain, Jean-Yves (1973). *Panjamon.* William Morrow & Company, IAC, New York.

Enriquez, C.M. (1927). *The Haunted Mountain of Borneo.* H.F. & G. Witherby, London.

Evans, I.H.N. (1922). *Among Pritimitive Peoples in Borneo.* Seeley, Service & Co. Ltd., London.

——— (1923). Studies in Religion, Folk-Lore and Custom in British North Borneo and the Malay Peninsula. Cambridge University Press, Cambridge.

Exodus 29: 10–12. Christian Community Bible. (1988). Claretian Publications, Philippines. p. 147.

Ezekiel 36: 25. Christian Community Bible. (1988). Claretian Publications, Philippines. p. 755.

Galvin, A.D. (1974). "Head Hunting—fact or fiction?". *The Brunei Museum Journal* 3(2): 17–21.

Hebrews 9: 19–22. Christian Community Bible. (1988). Claretian Publications, Philippines. p. 446.

Holland, D.C. (1962). Dusun Stories from Kota Belud. Whelan, F.G. (ed.). Borneo Literature Bureau, Kuching.

Jackson, the Rev. Thomas (1884). An Appeal—St. Joseph's Mission to the Head Hunters of Borneo. Dollard, Dublin.

——— (1884). "Letter in the Archives of St. Joseph's College, Mill Hill, London". 3 - C - 9g.

Kinabalu Sabah Times (1974). "Head Hunters' trophies are laid to rest". Kinabalu Sabah Times. Kota Kinabalu. 7 May, p. 10.

Lai Kwok Kin (1991). "When getting a wife meant first getting a head". Daily Express. Kota Kinabalu. 14 February, p. 4.

Numbers 19: 2b–4. Christian Community Bible. (1988). Claretian Publications, Philippines. p. 213.

Numbers 31: 21–23. The Jerusalem Bible. (1966). Longman Todd, London. p. 212.

Perry, W.J. (1918). *The Megalithic Culture of Indonesia.* Longmans, Green & Co., London.

Pius Kating (1989). "The Skulls of Sinsuron". In: I. Marsh (ed.). *Tales and Traditions from Sabah.* The Sabah Society, Kota Kinabalu. p. 51.

Ralon, Larry (2000). Skull in Four-Digit Ritual? *Daily Express*, Kota Kinabalu. 11 August, p. 1.

Rutter, Owen (1929). *The Pagans of North Borneo.* Hutchinson, London.

Sarda, James. (1994). *Time is up for 'living' skulls.* Daily Express, Kota Kinabalu. 11 September, p. 6.

Tregonning, K.G. (1965). A History of Modern Sabah 1881–1963. University of Malaya Press, Singapore.

Whelan, F.G. (1970). *A History of Sabah.* MacMillan & Company, Singapore.

Whitehead, J. (1893). *Exploration of Kina Balu, North Borneo.* Gurney & Jackson, London.

Williams, T.R. (1965). *The Dusun—A North Borneo Society.* Holt, Rinehart & Winston, New York.

——— (1965). "Tambunan of Dusun Social Structure". *Sociologus* 12: 142.

Wood, D.P.J. and Moser, B.J. (1957). *Village Communities in the Tambunan Area of British North Borneo.* Royal Geographical Society, London.

Woolley, G.C. (1936). "The Timoguns—A Murut Tribe of the Interior". *Native Affairs Bulletin* 1: 30.

INDEX

Other titles by *Natural History Publications (Borneo)*

For more information, please contact us at

Natural History Publications (Borneo) Sdn. Bhd.
A913, 9th Floor, Wisma Merdeka
P.O. Box 15291, 88863 Kota Kinabalu, Sabah, Malaysia
Tel: 088-233098 Fax: 088-240768 e-mail: chewlun@tm.net.my

Mount Kinabalu: Borneo's Magic Mountain—an introduction to the natural history of one of the world's great natural monuments by K.M. Wong & C.L. Chan

Enchanted Gardens of Kinabalu: A Borneo Diary by Susan M. Phillipps

A Colour Guide to Kinabalu Park by Susan K. Jacobson

Kinabalu: The Haunted Mountain of Borneo by C.M. Enriquez (Reprint)

National Parks of Sarawak
by Hans P. Hazebroek and Abang Kashim Abg. Morshidi

A Walk through the Lowland Rainforest of Sabah by Elaine J.F. Campbell

In Brunei Forests: An Introduction to the Plant Life of Brunei Darussalam by K.M. Wong (Revised Edition)

The Larger Fungi of Borneo by David N. Pegler

Pitcher-plants of Borneo by Anthea Phillipps & Anthony Lamb

Nepenthes of Borneo by Charles Clarke

The Plants of Mount Kinabalu 3: Gymnosperms and Non-orchid Monocotyledons by John H. Beaman & Reed S. Beaman

The Plants of Mount Kinabalu 4: Dicotyledon Families Acanthaceae –Lythraceae by John H. Beaman, Christiane Anderson & Reed S. Beaman

Slipper Orchids of Borneo by Phillip Cribb

The Genus Paphiopedilum (Second Edition) by Phillip Cribb

The Genus Pleione (Second Edition) by Phillip Cribb

Dendrochilum of Borneo by Jeffrey J. Wood

Orchids of Sumatra by J.B. Comber

Orchids of Sarawak: An Enumeration by Teofila E. Beaman, Jeffrey J. Wood, Reed S. Beaman and John H. Beaman

Gingers of Peninsular Malaysia and Singapore
by K. Larsen, H. Ibrahim, S.H. Khaw & L.G. Saw

Mosses and Liverworts of Mount Kinabalu
by Jan P. Frahm, Wolfgang Frey, Harald Kürschner & Mario Manzel

Birds of Mount Kinabalu, Borneo by Geoffrey W.H. Davison

The Birds of Borneo (Fourth Edition)
by Bertram E. Smythies (Revised by Geoffrey W.H. Davison)

The Birds of Burma (Fourth Edition)
by Bertram E. Smythies (Revised by Bertram E. Smythies)

Proboscis Monkeys of Borneo by Elizabeth L. Bennett & Francis Gombek

The Natural History of Orang-utan by Elizabeth L. Bennett

The Systematics and Zoogeography of the Amphibia of Borneo
by Robert F. Inger (Reprint)

A Field Guide to the Frogs of Borneo
by Robert F. Inger & Robert B. Stuebing

A Field Guide to the Snakes of Borneo
by Robert B. Stuebing & Robert F. Inger

The Natural History of Amphibians and Reptiles in Sabah
by Robert F. Inger & Tan Fui Lian

Marine Food Fishes and Fisheries of Sabah by Chin Phui Kong

Layang Layang: A Drop in the Ocean
by Nicolas Pilcher, Steve Oakley & Ghazally Ismail

Phasmids of Borneo by Philip E. Bragg

The Dragon of Kinabalu and other Borneo Stories by Owen Rutter (Reprint)

Land Below the Wind by Agnes N. Keith (Reprint)

Three Came Home by Agnes N. Keith (Reprint)

White Man Returns by Agnes N. Keith (Reprint)

Forest Life and Adventures in the Malay Archipelago
by Eric Mjöberg (Reprint)

A Naturalist in Borneo by Robert W.C. Shelford (Reprint)

Twenty Years in Borneo by Charles Bruce (Reprint)

With the Wild Men of Borneo by Elizabeth Mershon (Reprint)

Kadazan Folklore (Compiled and edited by Rita Lasimbang)

An Introduction to the Traditional Costumes of Sabah
(eds. Rita Lasimbang & Stella Moo-Tan)

Bahasa Malaysia titles:

Manual latihan pemuliharaan dan penyelidikan hidupan liar di lapangan
oleh Alan Rabinowitz (Translated by Maryati Mohamed)

Etnobotani oleh Gary J. Martin (Translated by Maryati Mohamed)

Panduan Lapangan Katak-Katak Borneo oleh R.F. Inger dan R.B. Stuebing

Other titles available through Natural History Publications (Borneo)

The Bamboos of Sabah by Soejatmi Dransfield

The Morphology, Anatomy, Biology and Classification of Peninsular
Malaysian Bamboos by K.M. Wong

Orchids of Borneo Vol. 1 by C.L. Chan, A. Lamb, P.S. Shim & J.J. Wood

Orchids of Borneo Vol. 2 by Jaap J. Vermeulen

Orchids of Borneo Vol. 3 by Jeffrey J. Wood

Orchids of Java by J.B. Comber

Forests and Trees of Brunei Darussalam (eds. K.M. Wong & A.S. Kamariah)

A Field Guide to the Mammals of Borneo
by Junaidi Payne & Charles M. Francis

Pocket Guide to the Birds of Borneo (Compiled by Charles M. Francis)

The Fresh-water Fishes of North Borneo by Robert F. Inger & Chin Phui Kong

The Exploration of Kina Balu by John Whitehead (Reprint)

Kinabalu: Summit of Borneo (eds. K.M. Wong & A. Phillipps)

Common Seashore Life of Brunei by Marina Wong & Aziah binte Hj. Ahmad

Birds of Pelong Rocks by Marina Wong & Hj. Mohammad bin Hj. Ibrahim

Ants of Sabah by Arthur Y.C. Chung

Traditional Stone and Wood Monuments of Sabah by Peter Phelan

Rafflesia: Magnificent Flower of Sabah by Kamarudin Mat Salleh

Borneo: The Stealer of Hearts by Oscar Cooke (Reprint)

The Theory and Application of A Systems Approach to Silvicultural Decision Making by Michael Kleine

Maliau Basin Scientific Expedition (eds. Maryati Mohamed, Waidi Sinun, Ann Anton, Mohd. Noh Dalimin & Abdul-Hamid Ahmad)

Tabin Scientific Expedition (eds. Maryati Mohamed, Mahedi Andau, Mohd. Nor Dalimin & Titol Peter Malim)

Klias-Binsulok Scientific Expedition (eds. Maryati Mohamed, Mashitah Yusoff and Sining Unchi)

The Kinabatangan Floodplain: An Introduction (compiled by Justine Vaz)

Traditional Cuisines of Sabah (ed. Rita Lasimbang)

Cultures, Costumes and Traditions of Sabah, Malaysia: An Introduction

Tamparuli Tamu: A Sabah Market by Tina Rimmer